LOCAVORE ADVENTURES

D0814404

LOCAVORE ADVENTURES

One Chef's Slow Food Journey

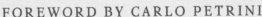

JIM WEAVER

FOREWORD BY CARLO PETRINI

Rivergate Books

an imprint of

Rutgers University Press

New Brunswick, New Jersey, and London

LIBRARY OF CONGRESS CATALOGING-IN-PUBLICATION DATA

Weaver, Jim, 1962–

Locavore adventures one chef's slow food journey / Jim Weaver ; with a foreword by Carlo Petrini.

    p.   cm.

  Includes bibliographical references.

  ISBN 978-0–8135–5170–8 (pbk. : alk. paper)

  1. Weaver, Jim, 1962 –   2. Cooks—United States—Biography.   3. Slow food movement—Middle Atlantic States.   4. Locavores.   5. Slow Food (Organization).   I. Title.

  TX649.W43A3   2012

  641.5092 — dc23

                                                            [B]
                                                   2011012785

A British Cataloging-in-Publication record for this book is available from the British Library.

Copyright © 2012 by Jim Weaver

Foreword copyright © 2012 by Carlo Petrini

Line art by Ellen C. Dawson

All rights reserved

No part of this book may be reproduced or utilized in any form or by any means, electronic or mechanical, or by any information storage and retrieval system, without written permission from the publisher. Please contact Rutgers University Press, 100 Joyce Kilmer Avenue, Piscataway, NJ 08854–8099. The only exception to this prohibition is "fair use" as defined by U.S. copyright law.

Visit our Web site: http://rutgerspress.rutgers.edu

Manufactured in the United States of America

R0433556084

CHICAGO PUBLIC LIBRARY

This book is dedicated to the family and friends
whom I have dined with on my journey,
especially my beautiful wife and travel partner, Kimberly.

Contents

Foreword

I am extremely happy to introduce Jim Weaver's book, for two important reasons. First, it tells the story of the Slow Food movement in New Jersey and, by extension, in all of the United States. Second, this book is an important sign that something extraordinary is happening around the nation, due in part to the influence of this movement, which I founded and lead.

Today we in the United States live in a period of great crisis, one that involves not only food, energy, economics, and the environment but also our values. Along with other observers, I am convinced that these crises do not represent the usual cyclical moments of difficulty to which we have become accustomed in recent decades. They are, instead, entropic, epoch making, and they will never pass if we continue to apply the same patterns and models that brought them on in the first place. To resolve these crises, we need new paradigms, new ways of thinking and acting that break fresh ground and that allow us to mix tradition with modernity, to combine what we know about the past with what we can imagine for the future.

I firmly believe—and I have evidence, thanks to the people who make up Slow Food and Terra Madre, a worldwide network of the food community—that these new paradigms are already affecting food and agriculture, as the media is starting to recognize. Edgar Morin, a well-known French sociologist and philosopher, is right when he says that "everything needs to begin anew, but everything has already begun anew." In the United States especially, I have seen a great change in the past twenty years. A robust, grassroots agriculture has emerged that is respectful of the environment and biodiversity. New forms of production have been introduced to both rural and urban communities. Microbreweries, fresh-milk cheesemakers, farmers' markets, and community-supported agriculture (CSA) illustrate how we are redefining the quality of American food while respecting the identity and the humanity of the people who produce it and choose to eat it. Such changes are an example for the rest of the world, for it is no accident that the strongest reaction to a global system of substandard food should have originated in the country that has given the greatest impetus to this twisted system. Slow Food's victory is a victory for the American people, who never cease to amaze the rest of the world.

Slow Food of New Jersey is one of the oldest branches of our movement, and as Jim's book proves, it has made a fundamental contribution. Therefore, my sincerest thanks go to Jim and to all the American members of Slow Food, past, present, and especially future. Keep striving, young people! Make the world better and more beautiful than it has ever been!

Carlo Petrini

October 2010

Translated by Professor Santi Buscemi

Acknowledgments

I would like to thank my staff at Tre Piani for working hard at the restaurant and giving me the time to write this book. I'm also grateful to Doreen Valentine and Leslie Mitchner at Rutgers University Press, who asked me to write this book and who are both foodies and Slow Food members. Thanks to everyone who agreed to be featured in the book, to those who don't even know you're mentioned here, and to the people who support Slow Food and take the time to search for great local foods. You are all integral parts of the story. I extend special thanks to Carlo Petrini for having the vision and the guts to start the International Slow Food Movement; without you, I may have never found my way. Finally, I thank Jean Torkelson, who listened to my story, read my drafts, and helped me shape my words into the book I had envisioned.

Jim Weaver
February 2011

LOCAVORE ADVENTURES

1

The "Ah-Hah" Moment, Slow Food Style

The International Slow Food Movement came into my life when I had reached a turning point in my career as a chef. I was looking for a path that made sense, although I was not sure what that path might be. But once I learned about Slow Food, my reasons for doing this work started coming together. I felt that I finally had a mission: to bring the best-possible food to my customers by empowering my environment to provide me with that food. At the same time I would prove that New Jersey is a gastronomically powerful place to live and work. In other words, Slow Food not only changed my life but gave me a professional purpose.

Getting involved with Slow Food was the first of my two best decisions. The second was to marry my wife, Kim, who has been my partner on our Slow Food journey and has put up with me as I've written this book. In our search for great food and the people and places behind it, Kim has been patient yet progressive, strong yet quiet. She has made me a better person, and the Slow Food movement has made me both a better chef and a better businessman.

Most of us have had "ah-hah" moments when something we've mulled over for a long time suddenly comes together. We turn a corner, and the answer is right in front of us. We glance down at a puzzle, and the dots connect. That's how the Slow Food movement came into my life: in one of those big, clarifying "Ah-hahs." As a chef and restaurant owner in the Garden State, I had long been frustrated that I couldn't directly purchase all the wonderful fresh foods that were being produced virtually next door to my restaurant. It made absolutely no sense that a locally farmed tomato had to be trucked out of state through a network of brokers and distributors, only to be trucked back to my door days later at three times the price and half the quality. In less than a week the tomato had been transformed from a fresh vegetable with a New Jersey pedigree to a hunk of anonymous produce that might have come from anywhere. I had always felt that one of my most important responsibilities as a chef is to obtain the best products that I can find. But how could I possibly know what is best if I didn't know where it came from? And here was another question that nagged: why had America allowed the noble turkey—which two hundred years ago was so robust that Ben Franklin had suggested that it be our national symbol—to become the blandest thing on the Thanksgiving plate, its taste overshadowed by everything from the gravy to the cranberry sauce? What had happened to the flavor of our food? These were the kinds of questions that were percolating in the back of my mind. But they only surfaced at the end of the long day, after the customers had gone and I was on my restaurant's front patio with my fellow foodies, as we riffed and griped about our wild and wonderful business over plates of antipasti and good wine. In 1998, Tre Piani opened in Princeton, New Jersey. I was the chef and a partner; later I became the sole owner. And although I loved the vitality of working in a major university town and was dedicated to bringing the finest-quality seasonal foods to the table, acquiring those foods was a constant struggle.

Then, about a year later, I got a brochure in the mail. I was about to chuck it along with the insurance solicitations and bonus-mile advertisements, but for some reason I stopped and took a good look at it. The brochure was from an outfit called the International Slow Food Movement. Intrigued, I kept reading; and as I read, I got more excited. It was answering every question that had ever bugged me about bland, artificially pumped-up food, not to mention explaining the country's outrageously expensive and complex Rube Goldberg mass food system. It suggested a way to make things better but without going the political route. Instead, Slow Food aimed to conquer the big guys by massing together in support of locally based growers, producers, and food suppliers. The object, in one of Slow Food's most familiar phrases, was "to preserve and protect local foods, local food traditions and promote a return to the dining table as a source of pleasure." I was excited and eager to know more. But little did I realize how much Slow Food would change my life.

The International Slow Food Movement was founded in Italy in the late 1980s by a group of food journalists led by an acidic and clever guy named Carlo Petrini. The organization marked the birth of a food revolution. In this case, the shot heard round the world was aimed at McDonald's, which was planning to open a fast-food franchise in the shadow of one of the world's most historic and beloved destinations: the Spanish Steps in Rome. Petrini was opposed to everything that had made McDonald's a global success and was determined to stop the iconic McMega corporation from selling burgers on those storied steps. Fundamentally, he and the other founders of the Slow Food movement objected to "the universal folly of fast life." (For the complete Slow Food manifesto, see the

Carlo Petrini,
founder of the
International
Slow Food
Movement

Photo by Jim Weaver

appendix.) They deplored nearly everything about our industry-driven, efficiency-worshipping way of life. Humanity may have invented the machine, but now we had become its slave.

Today there are Slow Food chapters in nearly fifty countries, and the movement has more than 200,000 members. Slow Food USA was formed in 2001; as of this writing, it has well over two hundred chapters, with more planned. My colleagues and I are proud to say that our chapter—Slow Food Central New Jersey—was the sixth to be formed in the United States. Slow Food was and is a resistance movement. But that doesn't mean you have to jump on Carlo Petrini's political wagon to support Slow Food. The principles of the movement can be taken to heart no matter what your politics. You can appreciate Slow Food whether you favor solutions from government or from free markets.

Each of you has your own beliefs about the way the world should work. But we share a universal trait: we all eat. And it doesn't take a Ph.D. in biology to understand that our bodies function best on wholesome, authentic food. As far as the best way to function in the real world, I think we can also agree that the most responsive societies function best from the local level too. That's why Slow Food is a movement for anyone who wants to support authentic food that's been grown and enjoyed as close to its source as possible. From that premise flows a whole way of life.

It's totally different from the pace of our Fast Food Nation, the title of Eric Schlosser's important book, which investigates the fast-food culture that has burdened our bodies with deceptively empty calories and hooked us on tastes and cravings that have been developed in chemical factories and "tasting" labs. People have been brainwashed into enjoying inexpensive processed food and beverage products and believing that there is nothing wrong with them. But even though the slick attorneys and marketers who represent the companies that manufacture and sell these foods may offer thousands of explanations for why their products are worthwhile, common sense dictates otherwise. The Slow Food movement aims to address these blights. Even better, it offers an actual philosophy and a plan of action.

The more I learned about the movement, the more enthusiastic I became. "Hey!" I thought. "We can do this!" So I contacted a group of people who I thought might feel the same way, and we decided to start a local Slow Food chapter. Attendees at our first meeting included a local farmer, a professional food writer, a wine expert, an agricultural marketing professional, and an extension agent from Rutgers University. (One of the perks of a meeting in the food business is that it's usually conducted over one heck of a great meal. In our case, the "meeting" was a four-hour lunch.) Several of the people at that initial meeting are still involved, and you will encounter them later in this book.

We didn't know it at the time, but we had just experienced another keynote of the Slow Food experience: conviviality. The movement consciously promotes a return to the table as a source of pleasure. Slow Food thinking helps us appreciate that many of the special times in our lives are spent at the table with family and friends, enjoying a meal and each other. It helps us realize that we need to push back from society's hectic pace and stress. As Carlo Petrini memorably put it, "There are two things that sustain human life. One of them is eating. Both should be enjoyed."

In this book you will meet the personalities who have made Slow Food a reality and have restored the meaning of conviviality. You'll meet George Rude, who is helping to bring back our true turkey heritage; Danny Cohen, whose traditional oysters leave patrons clamoring for more; Eran Wajswol, who started a cheese cave in his backyard; and Pegi Ballister-Howells, a protector of the heirloom tomato, to name just a few. Then there are the driving forces behind the movement itself: Carlo Petrini, for sure, and on these shores, Patrick Martins, who worked for the movement in Italy and then was assigned to bring Slow Food USA into prominence. Before we became friends, I called Patrick, then a stranger, to ask his advice about what we had to do to start a Slow Food chapter in New Jersey.

"New Jersey?" he deadpanned. (Wise guy; he's from Brooklyn.)

Where Do We Start?

Our group launched our first Slow Food event in August 1999. We called it Har-Fest, held it at Tre Piani, and invited local restaurants to provide free tastings of food using local, seasonal New Jersey products. To our surprise, the event became a spontaneous celebration that mingled dedicated foodies with curious members of the public—as if State Fair had met the Food Network. The crowd swelled to about five hundred people, each willing to pay a mere five dollars to help us cover expenses. We had a local wine tasting, music, and a seminar as well as a tasting of heirloom tomatoes. Everywhere, you saw local beekeepers and cranberry producers, tomato growers and cheesemakers. We had representatives from local food-related organizations such as the North Eastern Organic Farming Association and the New Jersey Mycological Association, dedicated to all things mushroom. I was overwhelmed by the number of different organizations that were representing food in New Jersey.

The media loved it. This was a big bonus since we had no real budget for promotion. But nearly every newspaper in New Jersey ran an article about Har-Fest. That day alone, we signed up more than fifty members for our new Slow Food chapter. Afterward, we all kicked back, with big grins on our faces, and hoisted our wine glasses. We knew we had accomplished something great, although we still had no idea what repercussions our success would have for us and for Slow Food. But by the end of the year, our membership had risen to well over one hundred members. Later, I was told unofficially that the media attention and the rapid rise of our local chapter had helped to convince the Italians that investing in Slow Food USA was a good idea.

Everyone Has the Right to a Good, Clean, Fair Meal

Many people think that Slow Food is some sort of elitist eating club. Nothing could be further from the truth. Simply, Slow Food is trying to restore a sustainable food chain, stretching from farm to table, that has not been in place for more than a hundred years. It's a system that produces the authentic, high-quality food that you and I need for survival. With this system in place, we will all eat better, have less poverty, and be healthier. Moreover, we will have less pollution, and the earth will have a chance to begin to heal itself. I really cannot think of anything more important.

But we still have a long way to go. Every human being should have access to food that is, in the words of Carlo Petrini, "good, clean, and fair." Yet most Americans are still entirely dependent on mass food production. Our wallets are being looted and our bodies polluted by big-business agriculture, genetically modified foods, pesticides, and growth hormones. The scary thing is that most people actually enjoy eating the processed, mass-produced products that fast-food restaurants, restaurant chains, and the like call food. Yet most of us have no idea about how that so-called food was made. If we did, we would be horrified. (Hint: just because it tastes like chicken and looks like chicken doesn't mean it is chicken.)

In the 1973 science-fiction movie *Soylent Green* (set in 2022, which at the time must have felt like light years away), fresh foods have become extinct, and the masses are forced to live on just one food product, called Soylent Green. Slow Food supporters see this movie as an important cautionary tale. Agribusiness is destroying our food system, and Slow Food encourages us to get angry. We need to take back our food supply.

All Smoke, No Roast

If you're aware, educated, and fairly well-off, chances are you're already making better food choices. You care where your food is coming from, and you have interest and empathy for the land and the people who work it. But most Americans don't have the time, money, or information to eat good food consistently, so they play right into the hands of corporate strategists and mass food producers, who are expert at modifying tastes in order to make inferior edibles seem satisfying. They know that heightened use of sugars, fats, and empty calories can make humans crave those fillers even more, and this is the dynamic that has fueled the multi-billion-dollar junk- and fast-food industries.

Many farms are also to blame. It's important to understand that not all farms are alike, although they all share the same cozy name. One of the tasks of Slow Food is to educate people about the huge difference between a small, local organic farm and a 100,000-acre monoculture farm. Today, most farms in America are owned by large companies with brilliant marketing strategies. They know how to build product loyalty and convince the masses that their product is delicious and nutritious. For example, a piece of much-touted farm-raised beef may in fact be genetically enhanced and artificially flavored. The phrase "farm-raised" might lead you to think you're eating something natural and healthy. But that may not really be so. An old friend of mine from Italy calls this kind of food "all smoke, no roast." And it's not just supermarket brands that fall prey to the hype. Restaurants do too.

Mommy, What's a Farm?

If we really want to do something positive about the future of our food, we must educate the next generation. The solution: teach gastronomy in our schools. But first, people need to know what gastronomy is not. It's not a hobby for the white wine and arugula crowd. It's not a secret society for fat guys. (And, please, somebody get to the kid who, when asked to define the word in home economics class, replied, "I think that's the study of gases in outer space.") A true gastronome is aware of the journey that food takes from the farm to the table. He or she understands the cause-and-effect relationship between inferior products and the environment. Most of all, the true gastronome sees how these dynamics may drive small, responsible farmers out of business forever.

According to Slow Food, gastronomy encompasses agriculture, ecology, sociology, economics, and more. In other words, it's about making authentic food and providing it to human beings at a fair price. Slow Food believes kids need to be educated about gastronomy while their palates are still being formed. Let's face it: the palates of those of us born after the 1950s have more or less been ruined. Fast food has inundated our lives. We're as familiar with fast-food restaurants, packaged treats, and sugar bombs as our ancestors were familiar with backyard vegetables and milk wagons.

But unless we consciously spread the Slow Food movement's ideals, the fast-food industry will continue its core strategy of marketing to young people. Kids will keep being lured by the promise of "a free toy with every order of fries!" After succumbing to that hook since infancy, is it any wonder that they grow up to be thirty pounds overweight and still craving those golden sticks of corporate grease? Cheap and prevalent, fast food creates problems that last a lifetime. Yes, fat, carbs, and sugars undeniably taste good, and the fast-food industry has cleverly built its success on enhancing these so-called comfort foods. We've even corrupted the appetites of wild animals: black bears, for instance, get so addicted to these products that they regularly break into cabins and cars to get at them. But what does this addiction tell us about ourselves?

There's no question that mass production solved the problem of how to distribute food quickly and hygienically to vast populations. But the food had to be modified from its authentic state, and protein producers still had to deal with the high cost of feeding and housing animals. Producers solved this challenge by moving animals through the system faster. Special chemically enhanced diets make the animals grow rapidly so they move into the food chain more quickly. But many of

My restaurant, Tre Piani, in Princeton, New Jersey
Photo by Jim Weaver

these chemical diets cause the animals to fatten up so fast that their bone structure can't support their own weight. Today's Thanksgiving Day turkey is a pale and
flabby ghost of its strutting ancestors. Did you ever notice that a Butter Ball looks
like a bowling ball?

Sometimes consumers feel better if they buy meat that's being advertised as
"fed on a natural diet!" But beware. This usually means a mixture of chemicals and
protein derived from bones and other slaughterhouse waste. Remember that "you
are what you eat" and think twice. Also remember that these poor beasts spend
their lives confined to extremely small areas. They live hard and die young and
never know what they're missing.

These problems aren't limited to livestock. For decades, seafood, fruits, and
vegetables have been artificially grown and chemically enhanced and sometimes
genetically engineered too. But if you take the time to investigate, you can find
many medium-sized and small companies that grow produce naturally and raise
their livestock humanely with plenty of living space and a nutritious diet. These
businesses care about how their products are treated and want a natural, sustainable
system that results in food that is good for the land, the livestock, and the people
who consume it.

So when you see an ad for "corn-fed beef," a siren should go off in your head. A cow's digestive system isn't designed for heavy corn consumption; it's designed for grass. Likewise, today's standard supermarket chicken is likely to have been fed pellets made from fishbones and marigold leaves to make the meat look yellow. FYI: real chickens are not yellow.

Stick a Fork in It

One day, as I was walking through a supermarket, I caught sight of a product so ridiculous that I could scarcely believe what I was seeing. Before me, on the shelf, was an Idaho potato wrapped in plastic, complete with microwave instructions. The price was one dollar. That's twice the cost of a potato in the produce bin.

In case you've had an impulse to make such a purchase, I offer the following recipe as an effort to stave off such absurdities and to drive a stake into corporate profits, one potato at a time.

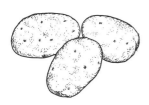

Microwave-Baked Potato

Serves 1

1 certified organic russet potato
1 piece of plastic wrap

Poke through potato skin with fork. Wrap potato in plastic wrap. Microwave for 4 to 6 minutes. When the potato is soft, it's done.

∽

But here's an easier and tastier method.

Baked Potatoes

Use that same dollar to buy two naked russet potatoes from the bin. Take them home, poke the skins with a fork, and bake them in a preheated 400-degree oven until the skin is crisp and the insides are fluffy.

∽

Why two potatoes? So you can invite a friend over. That way, you've fulfilled three major tenets of the Slow Food movement: you've eaten authentic food, you've paid a fair price, and you've fostered conviviality.

Now I'm going to suggest something that you may think is crazy, coming as it is from a chef and restaurant owner. Sure, I want to see you at my restaurant and at other family-owned restaurants where they care about what they cook. But I also feel strongly about this: learn to be happy by cooking at home. A home-cooked meal is a wonderful thing. You bond with family and friends; you create special memories. Around the family table, you can raise your voices, air family laundry, and belt out Uncle Louie's unpublished love ballads, all without worrying that you might end up on YouTube. Plus, it's the ideal place to put Slow Food principles into practice and learn to enjoy authentic food one meal at a time. Many of my own favorite memories recall events at our family table.

Even food failures can be unforgettable! My father, for instance, fancied himself quite the cook, though my sister and I had come to expect the worst. So when he invited me over for brunch one day, I braced myself. As I walked in, Dad was busy at the stove. My sister looked at me frantically, mouthing the words, "Please help him!"

Hmm. I looked into the pot bubbling on the stove. It was a mix of mussels and eggplant that had cooked for about an hour. The soupish concoction had been chased with a splash of old pantry spices and a dash of ketchup. Well, I'm too late here, I thought.

"We're having eggs Benedict too!" Dad announced triumphantly.

I looked into the dish where he was now starting to whip up his hollandaise sauce. At his side was a bottle of mustard.

"What's the mustard for?" I asked.

"That's what I put in my hollandaise to make it yellow," Dad said, as if this were the most natural step in the world. (Actually egg yolks, not mustard, give this classic sauce its color.)

My sister and I still laugh about that brunch. Mercifully, we've forgotten what the meal tasted like. But we'll never forget what it meant to have our father cook it.

Family meals, done right, are authentic Slow Food experiences, even when the cook's expertise leaves something to be desired. Your own kitchen is the only food laboratory you can really trust. A weird application of mustard? That's okay, and it might be light years better than many of the chemical emulsifiers that were dropped in your food thousands of miles away.

ᕽ RESOURCES

Slow Food USA
(888) SlowFood
http://www.slowfoodusa.org

International Slow Food Movement
http://www.slowfood.com

Tre Piani Restaurant
120 Rockingham Row
Princeton, NJ 08540
(609) 452–1515
http://www.trepiani.com

2

The Valley Shepherd Creamery

When you're working toward a goal, sometimes you have a big-picture moment when something happens and you say, "Yeah, that's it! That's what we're trying to do. We're on our way." That happened to me one late spring day in 2001. I was sitting on the patio of Tre Piani with a trio of fellow foodies, one of whom was involved in a startup chapter called Slow Food Northern New Jersey. Our group was holding an early organizational meeting for the chapter, which was the latest to join the state's growing and energized Slow Food movement.

Given our mood, "organizational meeting" sounds pretty straitlaced. That day we were all sparking off an irresistible mix of good food, good grog, and that sweet, frisky ache that springtime brings to your bones. Everything felt right that day: the right food, the right beer, and the right company. As we schmoozed, laughed, and traded stories, we tossed back samples from a local brewer and plates of Tre Piani's antipasti misti and fried calamari. No matter where the conversation strayed (for example, into the history of mead), we veered back to our theme, which was how to support and expand the links in our Slow Food movement. As always, that meant supporting local businesses and products in the tri-state area (New York, New Jersey, and Pennsylvania) that maintain a clean, healthy, and natural environment for both consumers and animals. It meant educating the public and inspiring their palates with the "real thing." As my favorite Slow Food motto puts it, "Live long—eat slow."

We already knew we were supporting quality products, locally grown, that people in our state could actually buy; and I was feeling confident about our newest chapter and the direction of Slow Food New Jersey. Looking around the table, I was proud to think how far we had come, with such quality leaders. One of them was Howie, an attorney and a serious foodie. As the man behind Slow Food Northern New Jersey, he had all the right stuff for the job. He's the kind of guy who knows all the restaurants and specialty food markets in the area. He knows who has the best pickles and which day of the week to hit the farmers' markets. You want a table at one of the trendiest good restaurants or to find the best cheese or the tastiest dim sum? Ask Howie. He's so well read and well traveled that I wouldn't be surprised if his computer had an alarm to alert him to upcoming food events and culinary-travel deals. I am always impressed when a civilian is truly in the know and has his finger on the food scene pulse.

Also in our merry band was renowned, award-winning food writer and restaurant reviewer Pat Tanner. Pat is the best kind of food critic: she critiques from experience. As a former caterer, she knows from the inside how hard the food business is. She has total respect for good food, has a great palate, and writes with flair and integrity. In addition to all of her professional qualities, Pat is a dear friend, and at that time she was also my co-leader at Slow Food Central New Jersey.

Eran Wajswol was yet another friend at the table. Eran used to be a successful real estate developer, except that he gave up that career to make cheese. His drive for perfection can be maddening, which is probably why his cheese company, Valley Shepherd Creamery, sells to some of the best restaurants in the country. Intense and driven, Eran has eyes that seem to pierce right through you, as if he's a father sizing up his daughter's first date. Yet look a little closer, and you'll see a twinkle lurking there too. He is, above all, a happy guy, especially now that he's given up his wingtips and pinstripes for a hair net, black rubber boots, and overalls with suspenders, his daily garb for churning out memorable cheese.

Eran answered the siren call of cheese with typical flamboyance. First, he decided to build a small cheese cave in his backyard in Tewksbury, New Jersey. But what's a cheese cave without the cheese source? So Eran imported a small herd of Friesian sheep from Belgium. Soon he had a state-of-the-art cheese-making facility set up next to his three-car garage, and there he was, running up and down a spiral staircase to his little cheese factory, happy as a littleneck clam. Next Eran tackled the challenge of creating cheese recipes, which led him, before long, to buying a farm in Long Valley, New Jersey. Today, Valley Shepherd Creamery is located on twelve acres of rolling farmland devoted to sheep raising, quality cheesemaking, and retailing through both Farmersville Cheese and the Sheep Shoppe.

On that spring day in 2001, with overachiever Eran Wajswol breaking bread with us, how could we not be talking cheese? His whole enterprise is dedicated to reintroducing the real stuff to American palates, which have been blighted too long by mass-produced imitations. Like the rest of us in the Slow Food movement, Eran is dedicated to providing quality food, naturally made and healthy, and

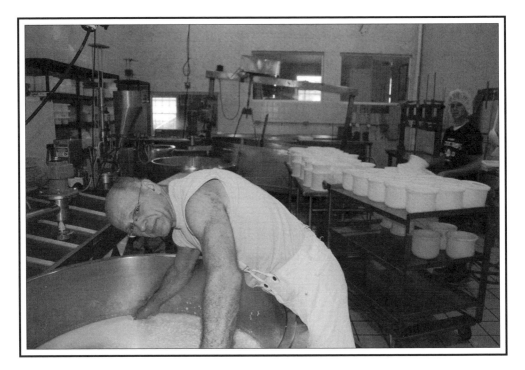

Eran making cheese
Photo by Jim Weaver

educating the public about his products. It's not hard to see why cheese captured his imagination. Like wine, cheese has mystery: its sum is bigger than its parts, as if nature is saying, "Here! See what you can do with this!" For wine, the starting point is the grape. For cheese, it's the milk. From that foundation arises a unique food group that includes tens of thousands of varieties, each with its own texture, flavor, and aroma. In the case of cheese, the milk might come from any number of animals. Most common are cow, goat, and sheep, but some cheesemakers use water buffalo or even yak milk. The results are nearly infinite—from the greenish-yellow Ragya Yak of Nepal, to the woodsy goat Banon of northern Provence, to Eran Wajswol's Bababloo, a blue cheese made from sheep's milk, courtesy of Morris County, New Jersey.

West Beats East

At some point in middle of our freewheeling afternoon, one of my servers approached the table. She said that she had a customer who was visiting from Italy and, as is the European custom, he craved a little cheese to cap his meal. What should she give him? Eran sat up as if he had just heard a fire alarm. "Here, let him try this," he said. Then he handed over a small chunk of his Pecorino-style cheese. Pecorino is a hard, salty cheese made from sheep's milk, and it has a proud Italian heritage. A version of Pecorino was a staple in the mess kits of Roman soldiers 2,000 years ago.

A few minutes later the server was back at our table. The customer wanted to know where the cheese was from. "Tell him New Jersey," I said.

A minute later, she returned again. "I hate to tell you this," she said, "but the customer is laughing at me. He wants to make sure he understood right. This cheese is from *New Jersey?*"

That was not the politic thing to say in this company: Eran whipped out his business card like a gunslinger pulling out his six gun. "Here, give him this," he said, adding a few choice words.

But moments later, our Italian visitor appeared on the patio, shaking everyone's hand and offering cheerful apologies. "*Mie scuse!* Forgive the mistake," he said. "It tasted just like the Pecorino made near my home in Tuscany."

Eventually, our satisfied customer left with Eran's business card, a standing invitation to tour Valley Shepherd Creamery, and (Eran being Eran), a final parting shot: "Hey, some respect next time for New Jersey, okay?" Then we all looked at each other, grinned, and raised our mugs in a toast: cheers to Eran's New Jersey Pecorino, now with a seal of approval from the home country! Our Tuscan customer had confirmed that Eran had accomplished what he'd set out to do: to offer the public memorable cheese of world-class quality that's been produced right here our own region. As for me, I was over the top. It was a proud moment in the history of Slow Food in New Jersey.

There's no doubt that great cheese can be made in your own neighborhood. Close to me, I have two favorite sources. One, of course, is Eran Wajswol's farm, and the second is Cherry Grove Organic Farm just outside of Princeton. Although Cherry Grove does not match the variety or quantity available at Valley Shepherd, it is making terrific cow's milk cheeses that just keep getting better. Slightly farther afield is the Old Chatham Sheep Herding Company in upper Columbia County in the Hudson Valley. It makes only a few varieties, including an exceptional Camembert. I'm also hooked on Old Chatham's yogurt and its fantastic blue cheese. I offer all of them to my customers at Tre Piani.

Unfortunately, great cheese is expensive. Some of the cheeses that I purchase wholesale cost upward of eighteen dollars per pound. But given the amazing variety of flavors and characteristics, the expense is worth it. You don't have to eat a lot to feel satisfied, nor do you need to use a lot when adding cheese to a recipe. If you're a lover of fine cheese, you know this instinctively: a grating of Pecorino over pasta or a few crumbles of blue cheese in a salad transforms the character of the dish. So pound for pound, an authentic, high-quality cheese really doesn't cost more if you use it correctly.

As for the mass-produced cheeses? Next to the real thing, these pallid chunks taste more like edible child's putty than robust and hearty cheese. It's why people with well-developed palates (like our new friend from Tuscany) have a hard time using the words "American-produced" and "cheese" in the same sentence. You can test this for yourself. Buy a piece of locally made cheese from a small producer such as Eran Wajswol. Taste it side by side with supermarket cheese. I promise you: the difference will be a revelation.

Even the Cure Came from France

How did we manage to turn one of the world's most distinctive foodstuffs into something that tastes more like bubble wrap? And what is the Slow Food movement doing to change this? For answers, let's turn to a little cheese history, mixed with some common sense.

Cheese has helped to sustain the human race since our earliest days. For thousands of years it's been a staple in diets around the world. History is fuzzy on its debut, but most likely the moment arrived as some prehistoric milkman or milkmaid was transporting fresh goat or sheep milk in a container made from an animal's stomach. Imagine that person's amazed reaction when he or she opened the sack: the liquid milk had vanished, leaving behind a pungent and tasty new food.

Modern biology can explain the phenomenon. Thanks to rennet, an enzyme that young ruminant animals produce in their stomachs, the milk had curdled, separating the milk into curds and whey, which are the essential components of cheese. Thus, cheese may be the oldest cooperative effort between animals and humans. Today we still need each other because it's impossible to make authentic, memorable cheese in a test tube.

The discovery of curds and whey occurred somewhere between 8000 and 3000 B.C., and most people who ate cheese thrived. Clearly, its good taste and nutritious qualities outweighed any unsanitary effects. (I wonder how many Roman soldiers were sidelined from the Punic Wars by iffy Pecorino?) But in the nineteenth century, the history of cheese got complicated. That's when French scientist Louis Pasteur invented a preservation system that killed most of the viable pathogens found in food. His 1864 discovery, which we know as pasteurization, set the stage for the scrupulously sanitized mass-food industry, but its most notable application is to dairy products such as cheese. This brings us to a key question. Cheese had an astonishingly successful run all by itself, long before Monsieur Pasteur got hold of it. So if humans have been eating cheese for more than 5,000 years and Pasteur's process has been around for less than 150 years, do we really need pasteurization to enjoy a good hunk of cheese?

First, let me say that I'm not against pasteurization. Far from it. (I don't hang out with the "flat Earth" folks either.) And it's worth observing that raw milk, the basic component of cheese, can be a welcome mat for pathogens such as *E. coli,* if mishandled. But nature has also given raw-milk cheese a defense mechanism that kills most pathogens just as effectively as pasteurization does: the natural process of aging cheese for at least thirty days. What's more, only raw milk can produce a cheese with true depth of flavor. In fact, most cheesemakers will tell you that it's almost impossible to make cheese with pasteurized or ultra-pasteurized milk.

Unfortunately, nature has been no match for American ingenuity and mass production. Enter the old standby that lurks today in most fridges: processed cheese. Processed cheese is a blend of ground-up cheeses that are emulsified (meaning they are mixed together by force) using heat and various chemicals. The process gives these cheese blends a longer shelf life, which makes them ideal for sitting in grocery stores or in containers for transcontinental travel. Chemically sanitized, processed cheese can be trucked across the country in vast batches. The chemicals also ramp down the pungency factor, which helps make mass-produced cheeses inoffensive to a wide array of taste buds. In other words, processed cheese equals better marketability.

Today, an argument is raging over processed versus unprocessed dairy products. At issue is whether raw milk—properly vetted, of course—should be legalized for large-scale commercial use. I don't want to get into the middle of this argument except to say that, from a chef's standpoint, there's no contest. Cheese made from raw milk tastes better in every way. I also believe that raw milk can actually be more wholesome than processed milk. Cheesemakers should at least have the choice of being able to use it. If it were more readily available, my job as a chef and restaurant owner would be much easier. I would rather give raw-milk cheese to my customers, and they would rather have it.

There are also other benefits to widening the commercial use of raw milk. For instance, I'm confident that high-quality cheese made from raw milk would cost less if it could be produced on a large commercial scale. Of course, the downside is that the minute someone in the production process messed up and consumers got sick, the backlash against raw milk could make regulations even more onerous than they are now. We already know from highly publicized incidents that it's impossible to eliminate contamination mistakes completely, even in tightly regulated categories such as beef or eggs.

Our consumer society has erred heavily on the side of caution, but such wariness comes at its own high price. By far the worst consequence of mass cheese production is that today we use gobs of processed cheese on our food. Cheese steaks, mozzarella sticks, cheese sandwiches: that's not what this noble foodstuff was meant to be! Talk about a catch-22: not only does processed cheese taste artificial, but its sheer artificiality leaves us unsatisfied, so we tend to eat more of it. Our appetite for inferior cheese may even have contributed to making cheese a villain in heart disease and obesity diagnoses. If American consumers were more familiar with the hearty, robust flavors of the real stuff, I'm convinced they would enjoy it more, be satisfied sooner, and therefore eat less.

In Europe, as our Italian visitor proved, several slices of choice cheese is the proper cap to a good meal, not the sugar bombs that often pass for dessert on this side of the pond. Cheese is a perfect balance between sweet and savory. It tends to settle the stomach. It's the last note of a great meal. The fact that most Americans prefer processed cheese is a triumph only for advertising and the mass food industry. Together, they have used technology and the power of suggestion to confound and confuse our sense of taste. It's as if they've scrambled our inborn nutritional navigation systems.

The Sheep Shoppe

At Valley Shepherd Creamery, Eran Wajswol and his family are fighting for real food. In keeping with the Slow Food movement, they are introducing the public to the startling, rich flavors of natural, organically produced cheese. Of course, Eran can't resist splashing his personality all over the operation. The creamery is a serious undertaking, but at first sight, it can look more like show business than farming.

All kinds of visitors, from families to bus groups, are welcomed. So are professionals, longtime farmers, and newcomers. The business includes a showroom, a farm tour, and retail store offering everything from kitchen tchotchkes to clothing to great cheese. In the Sheep Shoppe, browsers can buy sheep salt-and-pepper shakers, sheep's wool sweaters, and even Ewe Poo to fertilize their gardens. Cheese

Cheese ready to age

Photo by Jim Weaver

clocks, sheep puzzles, and sheep-related art line the shelves. For the tentative rookie sheep milker, there are lamb-nipple starter sets. And of course there is food: in addition to cheese, you'll find farm-fresh butter, pasta, ice cream, and yogurt in the refrigerated cases. In short, you can buy almost anything sheep-related here, including the sheep. But the heart of the enterprise is serious world-class cheesemaking.

In less than a decade, Eran and his wife, Debra, have turned Valley Shepherd Creamery into a sustainable farm. Their cheeses, made from raw milk, are available on the menus of many of America's best restaurants. How have they done it? They understand that technology, marketing, and diversity are key to their success. Eran's genius is that he combines modern technology with Old World methods, which he soaks up during his frequent trips to Europe. The result is an array of cheeses whose pedigrees go back thousands of years, and are good enough to fool a cheese aficionado from Tuscany.

One taste of Eran's cheeses and you'll realize you're not in your mother's fridge anymore. These cheeses are superb, and the variety is astounding. At last count, Valley Shepherd Creamery was producing more than twenty varieties of cheese and yogurt. It offers large and small wheels of varying ages and colors ranging from pale straw to red and yellow. It makes blue varieties and others infused with herbs and spices. Eran is so hands-on that, if you visit, it's likely he will be your tour guide. You'll see the sheep paddocks, the cheesemaking room, and the milking areas. You may be able to watch the herding of the sheep. Everything on the farm is dedicated to maintaining the great time-honored traditions of cheesemaking. But if you look closely, you'll also see that each sheep is wearing an ear tag that contains a computerized chip. From the information in the chip, Eran can track the amount of milk each sheep produces, which animals are star performers, and which are better suited for the barbecue. The Wajswols' business is a sterling example of how technology has moved beyond the mass food industry to the family farm. The creamery proves that small food producers can have access to cutting-edge methods—those that enhance the authentic product, not destroy it. Eran's enterprise proves that savvy use of technology can benefit his farm, the customers, and the environment. The animals have a happier life too.

Eran likes nothing better than showing off his farm to thousands of annual visitors and to prove to them that it's possible to run a business that is environmentally good, clean, and fair. Still, he's on the lookout for that one special visitor. Says Eran, a glint in his eye, "Can't wait for that guy from Tuscany to show up."

∯

Here are a couple of cheese-based recipes that I serve at Tre Piani.

Tuna and Manchego Cheese Skewers

Makes about 12 skewers

½ pound sushi-grade tuna, cut into bite-sized cubes
½ pound Manchego cheese, cut into bite-sized cubes
½ cup extra-virgin olive oil
1 tsp. crushed red pepper
1 tsp. sea salt
2 tsp. chopped parsley
¼ tsp. lemon zest

On toothpicks, skewer alternate chunks of tuna and cheese. Place the skewered picks in a single layer in a nonreactive container (glass or ceramic is best). Mix all the other ingredients and pour over the skewers; let marinate at least 1 hour or overnight. Serve slightly chilled.

Grilled Peach Salad with Arugula, Grilled Onions, Walnuts, Valley Shepherd Blue Cheese, and Crispy Prosciutto

Serves 4

4 peaches, cut in half and pits removed
1 small red onion, peeled and sliced thickly
8 large slices prosciutto, sliced to bacon thickness
1 large bunch arugula, well washed and dried
⅓ cup toasted walnut pieces
4 tbsp. crumbled Valley Shepherd blue cheese
2 tbsp. balsamic vinegar
¼ cup extra-virgin olive oil
1 tsp. sea salt

Heat the grill. Rub the cut sides of peaches with a little olive oil and put them cut side down onto the hot grill. Cook until the peach chars slightly, then turn them over and cool until they are warm through. Do the same with the onions, and then set aside the peaches and onions.

Preheat your oven to 400 degrees. Lay the prosciutto on a lightly oiled cookie sheet and bake until slightly crisp, about 5 minutes. Remove from oven, and set aside.

In a mixing bowl combine the arugula, walnuts, cheese, oil, vinegar, and salt.

In individual serving bowls, place each peach cut side up. Toss the arugula mixture and divide it over the peaches. Garnish each serving with 2 slices of crispy prosciutto and serve immediately.

く RESOURCES

Valley Shepherd Creamery cheeses are available at numerous farmers' markets throughout New York City and New Jersey as well as in many local restaurants and fine food markets. The website includes a complete list of products and where you can find them.

Valley Shepherd Creamery
50 Fairmount Road
Long Valley, NJ 07857
(908) 876–3200
http://www.valleyshepherd.com

Cherry Grove Organic Farm
3200 Lawrenceville Road (Route 206)
Lawrenceville, NJ 08698
(609) 219–0053
http://www.cherrygrovefarm.com

Old Chatham Sheep Herding Company
155 Shaker Museum Road
Old Chatham, NY 12136
(888) 743–3760
http://www.blacksheepcheese.com

3

The Delaware Bay Oyster

I'm speeding along a two-lane road in rural New Jersey, craning my neck for a glimpse of a bald eagle on the wing. The wetlands are lush with spring rains and teeming with eagles, cranes, and foxes. This wild and beautiful country would likely be a surprise to most Americans, who, thanks to generations of gangster films and late-night comedians, tend to think of New Jersey as a gritty urban pressure cooker. Yet the state is home to hundreds of farms tucked among rolling hills. Believe me, there's nothing ironic about our official moniker, "the Garden State." New Jersey once supplied produce and farm goods to the entire Northeast. Today we've gone a step further: now we also supply food to the world.

On this day I'm hunting for one of New Jersey's lost treasures—the state's once-commanding oyster industry. When Henry Hudson and his band of explorers arrived in the region in 1609, they looked out at 350 square miles of oyster reefs spanning the southern estuary that forms Delaware Bay. The region's Native Americans already were enjoying the oyster as a delicacy. From then on, it occupied the menus and minds of incoming settlers as well. Until the early 1900s, New Jersey's oyster industry seemed unstoppable. But by the mid-1950s, overharvesting, pollution, and disease sent the industry on a downward spiral. Although this glorious yet unprepossessing foodstuff never disappeared, its ability to sustain a great industry did. Yet there were already heartening signs of a comeback. As matter of fact, one big reason for my trip was to represent Slow Food USA and its ongoing Ark Project, whose goal is to save foods from extinction, just as Noah saved the animals in his ark. Slow Food Central New Jersey wanted our first national rescue effort to be the Delaware Bay oyster.

The Slow Food Ark Project is one of the best weapons in the movement's international arsenal. Slow Food members identify endangered foods from around the world in an attempt to save them from the mudslide of artificially made food. Our goal is to reintroduce them into the market or to open new niche markets, and we accomplish this by way of our national and international websites and

Baby oysters
in Cape May

Photo by Jim Weaver

through the efforts of local chapters. Our ark carries thousands of foods from around the globe, including rare sea salts, cheeses, beverages, seafood, livestock, fruits, vegetables, and grains.

In southern New Jersey, the oysters themselves are plentiful. Rather, it is the industry itself that is endangered, and our Slow Food chapter felt it deserved a boost. The region is home to two varieties of oyster. One is the basic Delaware Bay oyster, which is farmed on leased, prepared sea beds in the bay. The other is the Cape May Salt oyster, farmed on raised beds on the tidal flats that lie right off the beach in the town of Cape May Court House. Thanks to research sponsored by Rutgers University, cutting-edge farming techniques have increased the Salt oyster's resistance to disease and made it tastier than ever. I've kept it on my menu since 2001, and my customers love it.

On this day, I'm heading a hundred miles south to Delaware Bay, known for generations as New Jersey's oyster country. My goal is to visit two champions of the oyster. One is Danny Cohen, whose company, Atlantic Cape Fisheries, is responsible for the tasty and trademarked Cape May Salt oyster. The company has linked with Rutgers to revive the sixty-year-old "rack and bag" method of harvesting that makes these particular mollusks so special. But first, I'll stop to see Walter Canzonier of the Haskins Shellfish Laboratory, which is part of the Rutgers University New Jersey Agricultural Experiment Station. If you want to understand oysters and oyster country, Walt is your man.

As I drive, I can't help but chuckle at the complex and larger-than-life personality of my native state. Here I am, a man who works in a modern, Ivy League town, setting out to learn more about a one-ounce foodstuff that once supported an entire working class (and more than a few millionaires) on its squishy back. My guides will be two colorful guys who break all the stereotypes: Danny Cohen, a longtime fisherman who looks like a Ph.D., and Walt Canzonzier, a Ph.D. who looks like a fisherman. That's New Jersey for you.

Two and a half hours away from Tre Piani, I veer off the state road that zips me southeast through the Pine Barrens, where I pick up the Garden State Parkway, the final lap in my journey to oyster country. Soon I see a milky haze gathering to the east and sense a faint salt tang on my tongue, the first clues that the Atlantic Ocean is just over the horizon. Soon I'm passing signs for Ocean City, Avalon, Wildwood—names that, to people up and down the east coast, equal the summer playground affectionately known as "down the shore." But I'm not stopping at the shore, not yet. First, I'm heading a little west of the Cape May horn to Delaware Bay and the western beaches. This is oyster country, whose very nickname is a reminder that, until the mid-1950s, the phrase "oyster millionaire" didn't sound any funnier than "software millionaire" sounds today.

Soon I'm slicing through back roads across one of the most beautiful nature preserves in the country. This area surrounding the Maurice River in Cumberland County connects the Pine Barrens with Delaware Bay and is home to more than 50 percent of the state's endangered animal species along with the only wild rice stand in New Jersey. It's billed as the second-largest habitat for bald eagles on the east coast. Unfortunately, I never glimpse an eagle, though I do catch sight of a sign advertising an annual muskrat dinner at the local firehouse. It reminds me that many people in parts of New Jersey have a close relationship with local wildlife and depend on their own harvest for food. They are a natural constituency for Slow Food, and they understand its importance because they *live* Slow Food every day.

An Oyster by Any Other Name

Over the centuries, the undistinguished little bivalve we call an oyster has been celebrated in many lands. Well before Europeans arrived on the local scene, the indigenous people of Delaware, the Lenape tribe, thought of oysters as a gourmet food. So did the ancient Romans. According to one account, after Rome conquered Britain, the weary soldiers found themselves regretting that they'd ever set foot in such an uncouth country. Then they found an oyster bed, a discovery that led one homesick Roman to marvel, "There is some good here, after all!" In William Shakespeare's play *The Merry Wives of Windsor*, the character Pistol brags, "The world's mine oyster"; and writer Ernest Hemingway credited the oyster's

Oyster racks on the tidal flats in Cape May Courthouse, New Jersey

Photo by Jim Weaver

"cold liquid" for pulling him out of depression. The great American food writer M.F.K. Fisher sang its praises in her celebrated 1941 classic, *Consider the Oyster.* Among her priceless lines: "The oyster leads a dreadful but exciting life." That life was amplified by historian Mark Kurlansky in his lively 2007 book, *The Big Oyster: History on the Half Shell.* Kurlansky recounted the days when this deceptively dowdy shellfish once ruled in New York Harbor, feeding rich and poor alike and fueling an entire industry before it succumbed to the perils of success. Yet despite those hard times, this hardy, versatile mollusk is still found up and down the eastern seaboard, from Canada to Mexico, a chameleon that absorbs the unique flavors and textures of its own locale.

The Cape May Salt is a succulent, memorable variety of *Crassostrea virginica,* the family name of the Delaware Bay oyster, and I'm hoping that Walt Canzonzier will help me to understand how the Delaware Bay oyster came to dominate this region, where even the towns have oyster names. Consider, for instance, Bivalve, the town where Walt works. Bivalve is legendary: even a cursory Internet search turns up old photos of the town's sailing ships and toughened fishermen striding the docks. As I drive through Bivalve, taking in its odd-shaped houses and the oyster sheds lining the road, I feel like I'm stepping back in time. Bivalve, with its ramshackle buildings and sea smell, is exactly what I'd expect oyster country to look like.

And how to describe Walt? He's part scientist and part storyteller as well as one of the earth's foremost experts on oysters. A tall, vigorous man in his seventies, Walt has the ruddy complexion and deep-set eyes of a person who's on a first-name basis with tides and saltwater. His calm, settled look suggests a man at peace with himself. Wearing a red-checked woolen outdoorsman shirt with a pocket protector filled with half-dozen pens and pencils, Walt looks like he just got back from a fishing excursion with Hemingway . . . and took notes. His maverick persona belies the fact that he's one of most respected scientists in his field, with credentials that include project coordinator for the Maurice River Oyster Culture Foundation and president of the New Jersey Aquaculture Association.

End of an Era

When I mention the rotting docks and long-abandoned oyster schooners I've been noticing during my drive through oyster country, Walt nods ruefully. "Hard to believe, isn't it?" he says. "Those old piles of scrap used to be the guts of a great industry."

Like "king coal" in parts of Pennsylvania and the microchip in Silicon Valley, the Delaware Bay oyster brought boom times to Delaware Bay. For more than a hundred years, the oyster ruled here. At least 120 schooners jostled for berth in the nearby harbors and provided jobs for roughly 2,000 crew members. Shucking houses employed thousands of workers, and many more belonged to the supporting trades: foundries, sail makers, provision companies, inspection and transportation outfits, not to mention banks that readily accepted oyster futures as collateral on loans.

"A century ago, people would hang out in oyster parlors the way they hang out in pizzerias today," Walt tells me. "To European immigrants, oysters weren't considered a luxury, and definitely not some kind of high-falutin' gourmet item that they are today. Back then, the oyster was good, inexpensive food that even working people could enjoy. And once the transcontinental rail system was laid down? Then our oyster industry really took off. New Jersey was shipping oysters by train across the country, as far as San Francisco."

I detect a twinkle in Walt's deep-set eyes. "You know," he remarks, "it's said that the oysters that come out of San Francisco Bay today are the descendants of those Delaware Bay oysters—the ones that used to arrive by train, past their prime."

He sees my quizzical look. "Well, they had to be dumped *somewhere!*"

We can forgive Walt for being partial to the Delaware Bay's variety: at the time of our conversation, he had been in the business for fifty years, getting his start just when the oyster industry was starting its long dive. Back then, there were probably as many oyster recipes as there were families to eat them. That little lump of meat from the sea represented what a lump of coal or a lump of gold did in other places. It was a way of life. Now, however, there are only seven certified dealers left in the area, and only three of them handle significant quantities. Only one small shucking house is still in business, the last one in New Jersey. The oyster industry is a pale ghost of its past glory.

Yet nobody has told my customers at Tre Piani that the oyster's day has passed. The Cape May Salt is a perennial favorite, and other restaurant owners tell me the same. Its superior farming method, its versatility, and its taste keep the Salt in demand. It can be served in an exotic dish—for instance, baked *en glaçage* (in a light custard)—or eaten raw on the half shell with a bit of lemon or cocktail sauce. In general, the oyster's only drawback is people's perception that it's an acquired taste. As several famous wits have wisecracked, the first person in history to sample this "Ugly Betty" of the sea was one courageous gastronome. But neither Walt nor I have trouble seeing beauty behind the oyster's wallflower looks. Before I leave

Bivalve, I've enlisted his help in hoisting the Cape May Salt oyster onto the Slow Food USA ark.

At the time of my visit with Walt, Slow Food USA has yet to sponsor a food group on the ark. I want the Delaware Bay oyster industry to be the first. Realistically, Walt and I know that Slow Food won't be able to bring back the boom times and infrastructure of the nineteenth and early twentieth centuries. Our world has changed. But that doesn't mean we can't develop a good market for locally grown oysters of special quality, beginning with the Cape May Salt.

"Glad to be able to help," Walt says, as we shake hands. "Can't think of a better choice for your first project."

Cape May, Here I Come

Now that I've visited with Walt, I'm even more eager to meet with Danny Cohen in Cape May to learn exactly how his modern techniques are making this local oyster worthy of protection. A century ago, Cape May, the town where the fierce Atlantic bumps heads with Delaware Bay, was boomtown central for the oyster. Today, tourist beds may outrank oyster beds, but oysters are still an iconic part of Cape May. Now it's also home to a modern-day business that wants to bring great oysters back onto America's menus. To do that, Danny Cohen has revived a traditional method of farming oysters known as "rack and bag." This method, used more than sixty years ago, still produces the best and most consistent oysters, and Danny's company, Atlantic Cape Fisheries, has taken the lead in New Jersey industry.

Danny is a Cape May native and longtime fisherman, but he definitely doesn't come across as a stereotypical old salt. At first impression, he looks more like an attorney than a fisherman. His company runs several large boats up and down the east coast in search of many varieties of fresh seafood: sea scallops, squid, flounder, fluke, monkfish, tuna, and more. His fleet is one of the largest in New Jersey. Hardworking, shrewd, and insightful, Danny has been a key player in the resurgence of the oyster industry. His special contribution has been to reintroduce his now-trademarked Cape May Salts into the market.

As soon as I arrive, Danny and I, along with a few staff members, pile into a company truck for a drive to the oyster farm, which is located next to Cape May Court House, the county seat. To get there, we have to drive northwest from Cape May proper. After ten drab miles, we turn off into a trailer park and continue on through the rear of the park along an old dirt road peppered with giant potholes. All the while we nudge deeper into woods and wetlands. After about a mile, we

James Tweed, Cape May Salt oyster farmer

Photo by Jim Weaver

arrive at a hunting camp that seems to appear out of nowhere. This rough Brigadoon is outfitted with trailers, hammocks, coolers, and mysterious whirligigs. We trudge past the paraphernalia, and suddenly we're at the beach.

It's low tide on the western shore of Delaware Bay, and stretched out ahead of us are the oysters, thousands of them. They're nestling on a huge system of grids made of rebar (usually used to reinforce concrete), which is built onto the tidal flats. These cot-sized metal frames are lined up in rows upon rows of beds. Here, the oysters are allowed to grow out (that is, achieve market size) in black mesh bags. It's virtually an oyster dormitory.

James Tweed, one of Danny's employees and a lifetime waterman, dons a pair of waders and sets out through the tidal pools to fetch us some oysters. Right on the beach, he shucks a dozen or so and hands them around. Oh, the glory! Who needs cocktail forks, crushed ice, or dipping sauce? What's the point of white tablecloths and silver forks? We hunch around an old wooden table that looks as if it might have washed up from the sea. As for the object of our affections? The Cape May Salts kiss our palates: a perfect blend of sweet and salty, elegant and smooth. This must have been how the magnificent oyster tasted to history's first brave gastronome. To be with these guys on that scruffy beach, the tidewater stretching before us and glimmering like glass, the sea smelling tart and clean, while we taste the oyster in its purest form—what an experience. I am in oyster nirvana.

No Wonder They Ended Up at Princeton

As I've already mentioned, there are a two different varieties of oysters in the Delaware Bay. More common are what I call wild oysters: they're the workhorses of the species, a generic regional commodity that's farmed on prepared sea beds. These oysters are used for canning and other oyster-based food products, such as soups and stews, and you'll also find them breaded and fried. They can also be eaten raw and are often delicious, but they are neither as consistent nor as briny tasting as Danny's Cape May Salt oyster.

The Salt gets its name from the region's extra-briny waters; and according to Cape May lore, its pedigree goes back to the nineteenth century. Thanks to researchers at Rutgers University, Danny's revived version of the Salt is now disease-resistant. But what else sets the Salt apart from its more prosaic cousins? The answer is upbringing: Danny's approach to oyster farming is the key to this variety's consistent and outstanding quality.

In conventional oyster farming, which is limited to state-regulated zones, workers prepare the sea floor by dumping old oyster shells that have been dried in the sun and swept clean of contaminants. Next, they wait for naturally occurring oyster spat (baby oysters) to set on the prepared sea beds and cultch onto the old shells. The growth to market size takes two to three years.

But Danny's Salts actually begin their life in an onshore research facility run by Rutgers. Here, the microscopic seed is fed algae produced at the lab. By raising or lowering the water temperature, workers can trick the fledgling spat into faster growth at certain stages of life. But the process is still natural because no chemical additives are involved. Once they are about two millimeters long, the oysters are transferred to the rack-and-bag system that I have visited on the tidal flats. This method produces better oysters for several reasons. For one thing, the cyclical tides keep the oysters out of the water for part of every day, thus forcing the oysters to develop a tighter-sealing shell, which in turn gives them a longer shelf life. Another advantage is that they can grow to market size in just under two years. That gives the Cape May Salts a better cost-benefit ratio and makes them less susceptible to disease and parasites.

It's important to remember that more than one gift lurks under the oyster's homely shell. Besides the pleasure it gives to the palate, the oyster is also part of nature's cleanup squad. It's a filter feeder that lives off the algae that occur naturally in the water. A single oyster can filter about five hundred gallons of water every day. One waterman told me that in Delaware Bay, when the oyster production cycle is going full-tilt, water visibility clears to nearly seventy feet. That's why oysters beds are being planted to clean polluted waters around the world. Locally, they now grow around the pedestal of the Statue of Liberty in New York Harbor. But I wouldn't suggest eating them!

The Plan Worked

What happened to our bid to win our local oysters a spot on the Slow Food USA ark? We succeeded. The Cape May Salt oyster became the first protected food group sponsored by Slow Food USA. When asked, "Has Slow Food helped you?" James Tweed, Danny Cohen's oysterman, answered with an emphatic yes, telling me that production has since tripled and the demand has sustained itself. Once again, Slow Food has saved a food by eating it. Talk about a win-win situation!

I still savor my Delaware Bay adventure. With Walt Canzonier's invaluable help, we got Danny's incomparable Salt onto the ark. Then, to our surprise, the media in New Jersey, New York, and Philadelphia got hold of the story. Suddenly, the Delaware Bay oyster industry was back in the news and in the conversation, just as it was a century ago, when the oyster was king. Of course, we made sure that to offer Cape May Salts at our local Slow Food events and festivals. The crowd's consensus? "More, please!" Soon Danny's delectable product could be found in restaurants all over the tri-state area. Before Slow Food became involved, the not-so-dreadful and pretty exciting life of the Salts began and ended in just one place—Cape May. Today they are marketed through several distributors, and people from all over the United States and Europe contact me to ask about how to get them.

Occasionally, I'm able to slip away to enjoy the fare at somebody else's restaurant. And when I see Cape May Salt oysters on the menu, I smile and order a dozen.

Some Comestibilization Formulae
from the Cucina of Walt Canzonier

This chapter would not be complete without a few recipes from the kitchen of the great Walt Canzonier himself. I am not 100-percent able to translate his unique language but invite you to read between the lines and enjoy the recipes at your own risk.

· · ·

Bivalve-Flavored Baked Potatoes

Serves 8 to 10 people as a side dish

1 large Italian (*C. rossa*) onion, skinned and chopped fine
1 Cubanella pepper or small bell pepper, gutted and chopped fine
½ cup loosely packed celery fronds, chopped fine
1 pint shucked oysters
½ pound thickly sliced Polish ham, diced neatly
3 pounds red potatoes, well washed and thinly sliced
¼ cup fresh parsley, finely chopped, exclude the stems
Pinch ground thyme
½ tsp. ground black pepper
Salt to taste but no more than 1 tbsp. (may or may not be necessary,
    according to the salinity of the oysters)
3 tsp. flour (Wondra works nicely)
1 cup cold water
1 cup whole milk or half-and-half
1 cup bread crumbs from good bread

Laminate the solid ingredients into a shallow or deep baking dish in the following order: onions, pepper, celery, oysters (after checking for shell adhering to the adductor muscles, which should be removed to minimize complaints from eventual consumers), ham, potatoes. Disperse the parsley, thyme, black pepper, and salt (if needed) on the various levels during the lamination process. The order of lamination might opportunely be reversed on the second Wednesday of any month in which there are two full moons. Cover the dish tightly with plastic film and process in the microundulator (a microwave) at medium power for a period sufficient to partially cook the celery (approximately 3 minutes).

Now disperse the flour in the water by shaking it violently in a tightly closed jar. (Take care not to bump your elbow on an open cupboard door during this operation.) Remove the plastic film carefully, as hot steam can burn you, and pour the milk or half-and-half mixed with the flour suspension over the partially cooked mess in the dish. Lightly disturb the glop with a fork or a spoon to allow the liquid to infiltrate the mass and dispel any entrained air. Sprinkle the upper surface with a generous layer of bread crumbs. Place the dish (uncovered) on a piece of heavy-duty aluminum foil on the central rack of a preheated 350-degree oven and close the oven door. Bake until the juice bubbles thickly around the perimeter of the mass and the surface is nicely browned, between 45 minutes and

1 hour. Remove the dish from the oven, and place it on a heat-tolerant surface. (Unless you are a blacksmith, a clean folded towel between hands and dish is recommended.) Serve with a calibrated stainless-steel serving spoon made in Korea and eat cautiously with a four-tined fork. (It's a real tongue burner at this point.)

Ostrica Vive Intertidali
(Walt's Favorite Oyster Recipe)

Tools: Functional road vehicle or bay-worthy vessel
Hip boots or wading shoes (in warmer seasons)
Culling iron
Shucking knife (hinge-popper preferred)

Proceed to the intertidal flats of Cape May in the vicinity of King Crab Landing in time to arrive on the late ebb. Wade out on the flats to the location of the containerized oyster culture racks. Deftly using the culling iron, procure some two-year-old oysters from the populations that had set on the cull heaps and clean them of gross surface fouling. Caution: the growing edges of the oysters are razor-sharp and tend to inflict bloody cuts on the hands of the unwary. Holding the oyster securely in the palm of the hand with the fingers hooked around the bill, insert the shucking knife well into the hinge end and twist it to pop the resilient ligament that bonds the two valves. Sever the adductor muscle from the flat valve; scrape away any shell chips if present on the surface of the oyster, check for a valid heartbeat by peering through the pericardium, and then sever the muscle from the cup valve. Pierce the living oyster with the knife and convey it to your mouth. Take care not to obscure the natural flavor with abominable concoctions, as is so commonly practiced in the New York area. Masticate the oyster thoroughly to release the subtle essence that it has acquired by its sojourn in this ideal growing environment. Try another, and another!

☙ RESOURCES

To learn more about Cape May Salt oysters and other oysters from the Delaware Bay, visit these websites:

> http://www.slowfoodusa.org
> http://www.altanticcapes.com
> http://www.hsrl.rutgers.edu

To reach a local distributor of Cape May Salt oysters, contact:

Madison Seafood Company
(973) 623–8989

4

On the Hunt for a Hot Tomato

In 1820, as the legend goes, Colonel Robert Gibbon Johnson faced a huge crowd on the steps of the Salem County Courthouse in southwestern New Jersey. At his feet lay a bushel of round, ruddy fruit of uncertain origin. Despite its come-hither look—or perhaps because of it—this succulent crop had aroused citizens' suspicions. The fruit must be poisonous.

"Eat one! We dare you!" rose the cry. Whereupon the colonel brandished a juicy sphere, bit in, and promptly proclaimed it to be . . . quite interesting. You probably know from your own experience that the tomato is strangely compelling, with unique, indefinable qualities. At its best, the tomato is not quite sweet, not quite tart. Yet to this day, most people don't exactly know *what* it is. Vegetable? Fruit? Whatever it is, at its best, it's hard to beat.

This highly adaptable fruit, much loved by home gardeners and small farmers alike, thrives under the principles of the Slow Food philosophy, which promotes foods that are authentic, sustainable, and locally grown. Since Colonel Johnson's time, no other fruit has been so universally celebrated. Because of its balance of sugar to acid, it preserves well, and the natural flavors hold up so you can make a delicious tomato sauce in the dead of winter. It's a core ingredient in everything from pizza to chowder to veggie drinks. But unfortunately its versatility has also been its downfall. Taste and substance have fallen victim to mass production and cross-country transportation. Biting into one of these supermarket varieties is a little like looking up your first love after forty years and finding that, well, things just aren't quite the same.

Hurrah for the Rutgers Tomato!

Over the years, the Garden State has produced some of the most celebrated tomatoes in the world. Storied companies such as Heinz, Hunt's, and Campbell's have built their ketchup, sauce, and soup empires on New Jersey tomatoes. Yet what's been good for the mass consumption of tomato products has been rather bad for the tomato itself. That's why I embarked on this hunt. After all, I own an Italian restaurant, and the tomato is a revered ingredient in Italian and Mediterranean cuisines. At Tre Piani, to serve the best and most flavorful tomato is a matter of honor. But I was also partly driven by a more selfish reason. I might be a Slow Food advocate, but I'm also a restaurant owner with a bottom line to manage. I didn't see why I had to pay out-of-state costs to ship local tomatoes to Princeton. After all, I live in the middle of one of the premier tomato states in the country So I headed for the Rutgers New Jersey Agricultural Experiment Station (RNJAES) and Jack Rabin, the one guy who I believed could set me straight, has put considerable resources into restoring the tomato to its rightful role as a tasty food.

Back in 1934, RNJAES developed a variety called the Rutgers tomato, which lies at the center of our state's tomato history. Known for both its canning properties and its wonderful eating flavor, it became a worldwide best seller thanks to the cooperation work of Rutgers extension agents, New Jersey farmers, and major food companies. Today, the university is using its proven expertise to continue developing tomatoes that people really enjoy eating, and the man in charge of the job is as visionary as old Colonel Johnson was. But Jack, a research scientist and associate director of RNJAES, would laugh his head off at the label *visionary*. "I'm just the mouthpiece," he tells me. "My colleagues are the ones that actually do all the work."

Under his direction, RNJAES has instituted the Rediscovering the Jersey Tomato Project, which invites the public to come in and sample the tomatoes that Rutgers is breeding. Their opinions, duly recorded on official forms, are taken very seriously. The intent is to discover what the public wants in a tomato—taste? texture? bounce? And based on consumer reaction, Jack and his team believe they've scored big with the Ramapo tomato: "People who love the old-time flavor of tomatoes love the Ramapo." According to him, a delicate chemical balance creates the memorable tomato taste that most people consider ideal—a combination of degrees Brix (a unit that represents the sugar content of an aqueous solution), pH balances, and a naturally occurring chemical compound called furaneol. "I'm an old-fashioned Jersey tomato lover," he explained. "I want to feel that tartness in the mouth, along with the sweetness. Without tartness, it tastes flat and 'blah.' If it has low sweetness *and* too-low acidity, it tastes like cardboard." Clearly, the tomato has fallen into good hands.

Now a young-looking man in his early fifties, Jack became entranced with the tomato as a kid growing up on a New Jersey farm. That no-nonsense background

Freshly picked Rutgers tomatoes

Photo by Jim Weaver

combined with his years as a scientist and researcher made him suspicious of the Slow Food movement at first. He saw us as an elitist eating group dedicated to supplying food to the chi-chi clientele who frequented farmers' markets and expensive restaurants. But once he and I started talking, we found we were on the same side. The goal of both Slow Food and agricultural researchers like Jack Rabin is to give *everybody* access to food that's flavorful and authentic and produced as close to its consumer base as possible.

The Glory Years

Jack opened our conversation with a shocker. "You know, Jim," he said, "there's no such variety as the 'New Jersey Tomato.'" Now, as a chef and restaurant owner who pays attention to what I put on my table and serve to my guests, I was bowled over by the news. I had always thought that the New Jersey tomato (or Jersey tomato, for short) was a specific variety. But according to Jack, the name is merely the trademarked crop name of a one southern New Jersey farm.

On the other hand, a Rutgers tomato is the real deal. As Jack told me, "it improved upon the existing tomatoes because it was more uniform, and it did something very interesting: it ripened evenly, from the inside going outward. Plus, it had nice, uniform, glossy, smooth skin that was attractive. But most important, it was a general-use tomato. It was developed, selected, and bred for processing: to make tomato products and juice. It was so good for that use, and it tasted so good!" In other words, when people mention a Jersey tomato, what they're probably thinking of is the classic taste of the Rutgers variety; and for years now, the Rutgers team has been working to recover some of those original 1934 seeds.

The years just before World War II were the glory day of the tomato, and a good variety could make a huge difference in a family's finances. One famous example is a tomato called the Mortgage Lifter, cultivated during the Great Depression by a man known as Radiator Charlie. He sold each plant for a dollar and later bragged that his sales helped sustain a family of six, saving both his house and his business during tough economic times. According to Jack, "all the great tomato varieties were in fact general-use varieties, good for processing and wonderful for eating." The Rutgers tomato was a leader, but farmers also grew Ox Heart, Sungold, Boxcar Willie, Brandywine . . . the list goes on and on.

Today, restaurants, markets, and seed catalogs refer to such varieties as heirloom tomatoes. Chefs like heirloom tomatoes for several reasons. First, they are truly a seasonal delicacy because they do not have the thick skin bred into supermarket tomatoes so they can travel well and enjoy long shelf lives. It is almost impossible to get an heirloom tomato that hasn't been picked at the peak of freshness. Second, they come in a variety of shapes, colors, and flavors. Without much effort, anyone can slice a few, arrange them on a plate, and create a delicious and interesting dish.

There are many heirloom varieties of other fruits and vegetables available these days, but in my opinion none compares to the impact of a plate of mixed heirloom tomatoes. The flavors are intense: some are supersweet, others tart; some are soft, others crunchy; some run with juices, others retain them. Together, they are music in your mouth and a symphony of colors, shapes, and textures. All they need for perfection are a drizzle of great olive oil, a pinch of sea salt, and a touch of fresh herbs.

What Makes a Tomato Hot?

An heirloom variety is a purebred variety: that is, it has not been crossbred or messed with at all. Its characteristics are singular to itself and therefore unique. These are the varieties that have the highest risk of extinction, yet they also have their problems. As Jack points out, many of these much-loved tomatoes are also subject to horticultural defects—vulnerable to fungus, quick to rot. More important, "some taste good, and some not. People wax poetic about the good old days, but sometimes the good old days weren't so good." With the rise of mass production after World War II, agricultural researchers stepped in to solve some of these defects. As the tomato became commercially hotter, the race was on to improve yields, disease-resistance, sturdiness in transport, and standardization of color. For instance, rather than ripening naturally on the vine, as Rutgers tomatoes do, mass-produced tomatoes are subjected, when underripe, to ethylene gas and a controlled temperature drop (50 to 60 degrees Fahrenheit).

Of course, mass-marketed tomatoes and tomato byproducts are here to stay. As their supporters point out, mass production is what has made the tomato one of the most popular flavors in the world. True enough. But what about the rich, tasty, sun-ripened tomato that won over Colonel Johnson? That tomato is Jack's passion too. Like a wine lover at a tasting, he focuses on the details: flavor, texture, aroma, the balance of sweetness to tartness.

Right now Jack and his team at Rutgers are centering their hopes on the Ramapo tomato. Originally bred by Bernie Pollack, a former Rutgers professor, it was released into production in 1968. When its production stopped because commercial growers found other varieties more lucrative, home growers were upset. "We used to literally get Ramapo fan mail," Jack chuckled. "People were calling up—'Hey, what happened to my tomato flavor? Can't you bring back that old-time flavor?'" So with Professor Pollack's support, Rutgers reacquired the parent seed from a Japanese company, which at that time had exclusive rights to it, and researchers started working to bring back the Ramapo hybrid. Today it's once again getting rave reviews.

First, however, the new Ramapo had to be freed from the sins of its fathers while keeping the flavor. Jack explained his goals: "What I'm trying to do is find that middle ground, a tomato that's free from horticultural defects but re-creates that taste memory. The Ramapo fulfills that paradigm."

What exactly is taste memory? "You know when you eat a tomato and you sense that green, fresh, leafy smell?" he asked. "That smell is an organic volatile acid called z-3-hexanol. There are hundreds and hundreds of these molecules in tomatoes, and you remember them!"

As for taste itself, that's a factor that's also locked in the mysteries of chemistry. "You measure sweetness the same way in tomatoes as you do in wine—by degrees Brix," Jack explained. "That's the percent of sugar by weight, rather than by volume, and you measure it with a refractometer, the same way a guy walking out in the vineyard takes a reading on the wine grapes." He continued: "A typical tomato lover—which I consider myself and most of my friends—wants a tomato that is perceptibly sweet, and also has what I call a 'grip,' which refers to acidity. In wine, you call it 'tannin.' In other words, there's a hardness that tingles the side of my mouth and gums."

And this is the crux of the tomato problem: agriculturalists and researchers have developed varieties that tamper with the tomato's "sweet spot." Yes, modern tomatoes travel well across country and stay fresh in millions of cans of con-

Rutgers tomatoes

Photo by Jim Weaver

densed soup and pasta sauces. That's because these varieties have been bred to have higher acidity, which is a natural preservative. But that tampering is also the major culprit in throwing off the raw tomato's memorable flavor.

Jack told me about a celebrated research scientist, who upon nearing retirement, got to musing about how he had spent his career developing the big, glossy, firm, tomato varieties that processing companies clamor for. Now, in his golden years, the scientist had begun to wonder: by encouraging the genes that made for tomato firmness, had other genes been affected that were detrimental to the quality of culinary flavor? As Jack said, the guy had spent his research career "creating big, beautiful, disease-resistant plants and you can throw them at a windshield, but they have no flavor whatsoever."

The Plight of the Weeping Tomato

For millennia, humans have been playing with their food. This fairly natural process has helped humankind graft different grapevine varieties, develop cooking techniques, crossbreed cows to get the best milk, and even crossbreed species of dogs to be better hunters. It's a practice that is as old as humankind. Today, however, we also use chemistry to change our foods; and even more recently, scientists have begun to create genetically modified organisms (GMOs). Now that we can "mate" animal with vegetable, a real, live Mister Potato Head may not be far off.

The intentions, of course, are good. What's wrong with finding ways to make our foods disease-resistant, healthier, and easier to grow in places that are short of food? But there's also another question: what will be the long-term repercussions to our health and the planet's biodiversity? For instance, consider a variety of corn that contains a gene that effectively gives it the ability to make its own pesticide. In other words, the corn is able to kill bugs from the inside out. That sounds like a great way to grow a big crop, but it doesn't do much for my appetite.

Over the years, the ideal eating tomato—pliable yet firm, tender to the touch, and just sweet enough—has given way to a harder tomato that travels well, resists disease and decay, and multiplies like a rabbit. Why? Because, Jack said, "the guy who buys for the supermarket chain doesn't want bruised, broken, or weeping tomatoes—that's money lost." But researchers forgot to consult the consumer. "We were following a paradigm, but we weren't asking the public what they wanted. We were developing a very successful product that, it turns out, was making tomato lovers unhappy. There was no conspiracy—it's just that 'making them happy' wasn't what we were directed to do!"

Today, as a seasoned researcher and tomato aficionado, Jack can see the big picture. But when he was a young researcher, the established paradigm was "we need tomatoes that won't turn into a bag of mush between California and Chicago." He shared a story about a celebrated researcher in California who arranged to have tomato fields planted near a hardtop road. Researchers would pluck the tomatoes, walk over to the road, and drop them on the pavement. The conclusion was as simple as the procedure: if it didn't break, it was a better tomato. Another researcher, critical of that relaxed, unscientific California method, resolved to improve on it. His solution, Jack said, was to line up his tomatoes in a rain gutter ("that's what made it scientific"), set the trough three feet off the ground, and then flip it over. The tomatoes that didn't break survived to be rebred. But "who the hell was tasting them? Nobody told us to taste them. . . . That wasn't the target!"

Out of the Gutter and Back to the People

Science was very different in 1934, when Rutgers research scientist and breeder Lyman Schermerhorn introduced the Rutgers tomato, which became, according to the university's website, "the preferred choice of seventy-five percent of commercial growers for the remainder of the twentieth century, with worldwide use." That's because, as Jack explained, "it had high yield, smooth flesh, resisted disease, and also had a wonderful flavor." How did Schermerhorn manage to pack durability *and* flavor into one tomato? "He was also eating the damn things!"

Today, Schermerhorn's legacy is alive and well in the Rutgers-bred Ramapo tomato. When Jack and his team members see the ordinary people who take part in the taste-test process light up at their first taste of the Ramapo, they feel something akin to a spiritual experience. "This rediscovering of the 'Jersey Tomato' was an epiphany for me," Jack said. "I had people tell me, 'What you folks are doing as researchers is empowering me as an eater and a tomato lover.' I have to say, in agricultural research, we never had that kind of reaction before. We're inviting ordinary people, not just farmers with their boots on, to come out to our research farms and sample our tomatoes. These are people passionate about tomatoes." He added, "People are writing thank-you letters saying, '*This* is the tomato I remember!'"

I thought, "Wow, this really does bring everything full circle." Almost two hundred years ago, a cocky New Jersey colonel tasted a tomato, a symbolic first step toward making the state one of the great tomato centers of the world. Our own state university, Rutgers, has been instrumental at making the tomato universally popular, whether in its raw state or as one of the most common ingredients in the world. Now, in the twenty-first century, a Rutgers scientist named Jack Rabin is restoring the original goodness of this food. And along comes the Slow Food movement, joining with Rutgers to ensure that this state treasure continues to thrive on New Jersey farms and can be enjoyed locally, everywhere, on our dining tables and in our menus.

Before we parted, Jack and I talked about how good it has been to find this common ground. We're glad to know we're united in our love for food that's authentic and natural, that's "good, clean, and fair"— in particular, this great New Jersey food, the tomato. But I also learned that Slow Food needs to do more than just educate the public. It also needs to educate the educators. "You know, Jim, maybe this is profound," Jack said. "What you and the Slow Food movement are doing—you're all about human beings having a different kind of connection to their food. For the first time, chefs like you, and researchers like me, are inviting human beings to have an equal say along with the rain gutter." That kind of thinking can really change the world!

☞

Following are a couple of tomato recipes from Tre Piani, plus a recipe from Will Mooney of the Brothers Moon Restaurant.

Pasta with Heirloom Tomato Sauce

Serves 4

1 pound pasta
⅓ cup extra-virgin olive oil
4 cloves garlic, thickly sliced
1 tsp. crushed red pepper
2 cups chopped fresh heirloom tomatoes
2 tbsp. chopped fresh parsley
2 tbsp. torn fresh basil
Sea salt

Bring a large pot of lightly salted water to a boil and add the pasta. Cook according to the package instructions. Meanwhile, heat the olive oil in a large skillet over a medium flame. Add the garlic, and cook until lightly browned. Add the crushed pepper and the tomatoes. Cook over high heat until the tomatoes break down and thicken slightly, 5 to 8 minutes depending on how watery the tomatoes are. Add the parsley and basil, and season with salt. Drain the pasta well, and toss with the sauce.

Zuppa di Mozzarella

Serves 4

½ cup extra-virgin olive oil
3 cloves garlic, thinly sliced
1 tsp. crushed red pepper
2 pounds fresh New Jersey–grown tomatoes, peeled and seeded, and chopped
1 tbsp. chopped fresh parsley
1 tbsp. chopped fresh basil
2 tsp. kosher salt
4 1-ounce pieces freshly made mozzarella

Heat two-thirds of the olive oil in a large sauce pan over medium heat. Add the sliced garlic, and cook slowly until lightly browned. Add the crushed red pepper and the tomatoes. Let the sauce cook until it begins to thicken, which should take 10 to 15 minutes. Season with the parsley, basil, and salt. The consistency should be somewhere between soup and sauce.

Place one piece of mozzarella in each serving bowl, and pour the hot sauce over it. Drizzle with the remaining olive oil and serve immediately.

Sliced Heirloom Tomatoes with Fennel and Cucumber

Will Mooney, the Brothers Moon Restaurant

Serves 4

½ lemon, peeled and segmented
1 ounce extra-virgin olive oil
½ tbsp. shallots
2 heirloom tomatoes, sliced
½ head fennel, sliced very thin
½ cucumber, peeled, seeded, and sliced very thin
Coarse sea salt
Freshly ground black pepper

For the dressing, puree the lemon segments with olive oil and shallots. (This can be done 3 to 4 days in advance.)

Arrange tomatoes on a plate. Toss the fennel and cucumber with half the dressing and place on top of the tomatoes. Drizzle the remaining dressing onto the plate. Season to taste with salt and pepper.

❧ RESOURCES

Visit here to learn more about the Rediscovering the Jersey Tomato Project or to purchase Rutgers tomato seeds:

http://www.njfarmfresh.rutgers.edu/JerseyTomato.html

To find heirloom seeds for just about anything, visit the Seed Savers Exchange:

http://www.seedsavers.org

5

The Griggstown Quail Farm

George Rude is a tall, burly man—a rough-and-tumble Vietnam veteran who prizes his gun collection, his trophy heads, and a plain, commonsense manner. Regular visitors to his farm still chuckle about the prim visitor from the city who paused during a tour to complain that a fly had just wafted across her line of sight. In response, George barked, "Well, ma'am, this is a farm. What do you *expect* flies to do?" At first glance you wouldn't peg him as a champion of the Slow Food movement or guess that he had won the admiration of James Beard, one of America's greatest food critics. Yet under George's leadership, Griggstown Quail Farm and Market supplies tens of thousands of birds every year to fine restaurants, specialty vendors, and markets throughout the tri-state area. During the past three decades, George has become a giant in the New Jersey Slow Food community, and his farm has become a go-to destination for supporters of healthy, locally grown food that's produced humanely and naturally.

George's farm has long been popular among restaurant owners, chefs, and supporters of local food. But he wanted to reach out to the general public as well. So in 2004, as a way to celebrate Griggstown Farm's "field to market" theme, he began hosting the All Bird Barbecue, with sponsorship support from Slow Food Central New Jersey. Staffs from Griggstown and Tre Piani prepared food for the extensive buffet, while local wineries supplied the libations. For three years in a row we were blessed with perfect picnic days, and hundreds of people paid admission to celebrate George's food and explore his terrain. They took hay-wagon tours, mingled, and enjoyed live music. They feasted on free-range chicken (peach-glazed or fried), smoked quail, rotisserie poussin, duck sausages, Jersey tomatoes, sweet corn, salads, and freshly made pies. Held in the slanting harvest light of autumn, these were magical events. We were elbow-to-plate in a crowd of guests, surrounded by tables of delicious food. The air was thick with aromas, music, and laughter. We believed this new Slow Food tradition might last for years to come.

Then an ugly incident forced George to stop the party. One night in 2006, several weeks after the last All Bird Barbecue, animal-rights activists broke into the farm and tore down the fences and netting that enclose the vast pens where the free-range birds live. Their malicious actions resulted in thousands of dollars' worth of damage. Later, George learned that the offenders had actually come to the barbecue posing as guests so they could take the tour and learn the lay of the land. They hadn't just been dishonest and cowardly, but they had also breached the farm's hospitality. I understand that these activists believed that they were acting on behalf of the birds and that it is inhumane to raise any animal for food. In truth, however, without George's commitment to them, the birds would probably not have had any life at all.

At the Griggstown Farm, the birds are treated humanely and have lots of room to roam and stretch their legs and wings. They have access to high-quality feed and water twenty-four hours every day and live happily in a natural environment. Compare their lives to the miserable existence of the millions of Perdue- and Tyson-grown chickens who end up in supermarkets and fast-food restaurants. Imagine living in a wire crate so small that you cannot turn around. Your cage is one of 100,000 or so, arranged in stacks of thirty in a row a quarter-mile long. Your food and water appear mechanically on a conveyor belt. Your diet is made from processed corn, soybeans, fillers, chemicals, antibiotics, growth hormones, artificial coloring agents, and other secret ingredients. The ammonia smell of the feces is so powerful that workers wear gasmasks in order to perform their jobs. Your flesh grows so much faster than your bones that you can barely stand. At about eight weeks of age, you are big enough for the market, so you are quickly electrocuted and hung upside down on another conveyor belt, where the blood runs from your body and the bodies of your 100,000 colleagues. You are then gutted with a powerful vacuum and soaked in a blood, water, and chemical solution to cleanse you. Eventually you are chilled, bagged, and shipped far away from where you spent your short life.

That's not how the birds live on George's farm, but animal-rights activists targeted him anyway. And thanks to their ignorance, the birds they "liberated" all died. These animals had never had to fend for themselves in the wild. They didn't know how to find food or water. They certainly didn't know how to survive predators such as foxes and coyotes. The incident was a thoughtless act of destruction. Yet George didn't rant about the outrage or undertake extensive security measures. That's not his style. He just shut down the barbecue. We did, however, hear rumors that he'd made a few choice comments about activists who didn't have the guts to storm the electric fences of Perdue and Tyson.

The Rudes : George, Joan, and Chip

Photo by Matt Sytsema

Going Down the Road

One afternoon, as I drove alongside the Delaware and Raritan Canal heading for a visit with George, I found myself reflecting on the activist incident. Clearly, people still need to be educated about good, healthy food and humane food production. Even many of those who claim to be on the side of the animals don't have a clue. Yet despite my worried thoughts, the drive to Griggstown Farm evoked an air of peace, tradition, and openness, just as the farm itself did. The narrow, winding canal road is always lush with green leaves and vines, even in winter. It's a very old road, with a long history. Beginning in the 1700s, it was used as a causeway for freight, and later it became a route for Civil War troops moving south. Even today, two modern cars driving on the canal road can barely fit side by side. Old stone fences define property boundaries, and the road is lined with old stone homes and red barns. Often, a murky fog hangs low over the adjacent canal.

I always know I'm getting close to the farm when I start seeing a pheasant or two. And then I catch sight of the sign welcoming the public to the farm's retail store on Bunkerhill Road. The store, which was added in 2003, employs both a chef and a pastry chef, and visitors can watch them at work through the large kitchen window. The chef, Matt Sytsema, is young, talented, and enthusiastic. Every day, he and his team churn out dozens of homemade pies, cookies, pot pies, sausages, soups, and rotisserie-roasted birds that are for sale in the store. Raised on a dairy farm, Matt trained at the Culinary Institute of America and is dedicated to farm-fresh foods. Visitors beat a path to the door for his signature chicken pot pie.

You can also purchase many varieties of birds there: chickens, turkeys, ducks, geese, and, of course, quail. The store offers quail eggs and fresh produce as well as products from D'Artagnan, a New Jersey company that prepares and sells Hudson Valley foie gras, pâtés, and other game meats. In the midst of the daily hum, visitors are likely to catch sight of George's crusty yet cheery presence. If he's not there, he's probably off somewhere on his hundred or so acres, maybe bow-hunting for coyotes. But when I arrived, he was ready and waiting.

"Hi, George!" I said. "How's business?"

He looked fierce. "Aw, can't make no damn money in farming no more. The price of feed is through the roof. Bud, you tell me this—how the heck am I supposed to make money when I got to pay for the feed, kill the birds, dress the birds, deliver the birds, and nobody wants to pay what I need to get for them?"

Yet for all his grousing, I suspect that George wouldn't have it any other way. He plays the part of tough old farmer, but those who know him understand that both his soft heart and his canny brain for business recognized that working with Slow Food was a good idea. That's not to say that George dived into bed with the movement all at once. He started the farm in 1973 as a way to supply quail to neighboring hunters, including himself. Word got around to a local chef, and from there the news spread to James Beard, who was ahead of his time as a champion of naturally and locally grown foods. Eventually, Beard tasted a Griggstown bird, and he gave it the equivalent of a five-star review. Even better, he asked George if he would consider selling his quail to New York City restaurants. George agreed, and the rest is history. Today, Griggstown Quail Farm is USDA certified and operates with a fleet of trucks and a network of quality food purveyors. The Rudes, including George's wife, Joan, and their son, George Jr., work on the farm along with other staff members, while George's younger brother Peter delivers to a round of New Jersey restaurants and then doubles back to work on the farm too.

Let's Talk Turkey

Several years ago, I set out to convince George to participate in Slow Food USA's national Ark Project to save four endangered breeds of turkeys. Our mission was to coax back from near-extinction a quartet of America's most historic breeds: the Narragansett, the Bourbon Red, the Jersey Buff, and the Standard Bronze. Slow Food USA asked sixty farmers across the country to raise one hundred each of these endangered breeds, on the understanding that Slow Food would presell them and thus effectively guarantee the sales. In gruff George Rude fashion, he reluctantly agreed to take part. But by then I knew George, and I understood he was just as excited as the rest of us were about the Heritage Breed Turkey Project. As a matter of fact, I'd heard through the Slow Food network (George never trumpets these things himself) that he had actually released a few of these grand birds back into their original wild habitat. His act wasn't equivalent to the inept do-gooderism of slick urban activists. Nor did it reveal a man who was lusting after a solid bottom-line profit. It was the act of someone who wanted to see a breed survive.

As George and all of us in the Slow Food Movement know, these breeds sorely need our help. The villain here is efficiency—a weapon as lethal as one of George's .22s. These beautiful breeds are struggling to survive purely because of financial reasons. As a return on investment, the Heritage breeds will lose every time because they require twice as much feed to get ready for market, which is the most expensive part of the business. Moreover, they take twice as long to raise and never get as big as their lumbering cousin, the Broad-Breasted White, which is why it's the main guest at most Thanksgiving tables.

Now, I have nothing against the White, except that it's been developed in laboratories instead of by farmers. The breed's claim to fame is that it takes only about three months to raise. Yet if you ever get the opportunity to taste the genuine thing, I guarantee you'll never go back, even if you have to pay more. When you watch these magnificent Heritage birds in action, you can understand why Ben Franklin believed they should be our national bird. Flaunting their beautiful, colorful plumage, they run and fly around their pens on George's farm. They are loud and proud and advertise it. These are the turkeys of yesteryear, turkeys that are truly fitting as the centerpiece of a feast. The meat is firm and moist. The flavor is rich with a hint of gaminess and finesse not found in the supermarket variety. It's like the difference between a loaf of squishy white bread and a loaf of crusty homemade bread, just sprung from the oven.

Unfortunately, generations of Americans have grown up with the pale and waddling White. These turkeys can't fly because they have been bred to grow so fat that their wings will not support their weight. Sure, on George's farm, they have as much freedom as the Heritage birds do, but all they can manage is to lurch

Preparing chicken pot pie at Griggstown Quail Farm
Photo by Matt Sytsema

around the yard. They can't even reproduce. The Whites are born and bred to be better dead than alive. So why does George raise them? The brutal answer is that he has to in order to compete. In contrast to the few hundred or so rare breeds he raises, George raises thousands of these artificially plumped-up birds. This is what the market wants. Moreover, their cost is one-quarter of the price of the Heritage breeds. Still, George being George, he makes sure his Whites are fed better and raised more humanely than any average supermarket Butterball. After all, it's not their fault—or his—that they are condemned to exist from egg to table with virtually no meaningful life in between. George puts it this way: "Bud, I got to sell 2,000 whites to pay for the feed, and then I still got to do the markets!"

Yet things are changing for the better. Little by little, the Slow Food philosophy is affecting more menus and dinner tables. Thanks to George and the other farmers, during the first year of our Heritage Breed Turkey Project, Slow Food USA sold every turkey. The following year all of the farmers participated again, and they have done so every year since. By the second year, we won a major victory when the American Livestock Breeds Conservancy changed the status of three of the endangered breeds from "critical" to "watch." The trend is clear: we are effectively saving a species by eating them! Today, several years after the program began, the Griggstown Quail Farm is raising 500 to 1,000 Heritage breed turkeys annually.

Bird-Brained

Over the years, I have cooked many of George's birds at Tre Piani, and all of them have been delicious. Yet I'm always asking myself, "Am I the only person in the restaurant who can taste the difference?" My business side says, "Don't spend money on his chickens when you can buy mass-produced chickens for a quarter of the price." But my chef side says, "Your guests will love them, and your staff will be proud of the quality."

Chicken poses a special problem. Thanks to fast food, Americans have learned to crave either boneless, skinless chicken breasts or nuggets made of odds and ends that have been breaded and deep-fried beyond recognition. If, as a chef and a business owner, I can only serve breast meat to my customers, what do I do with the rest of the chicken? For a humanely raised whole chicken, I'm likely to pay $2.50 per pound. So if I don't use the entire chicken, I'm throwing away money. But if I choose to buy chicken from the big companies, I pay about $1.50 per pound for breast meat that's already been skinned and boned and requires almost no labor from me. Mass-produced whole chickens may cost only fifty cents per pound— five times less than George's humanely raised birds cost. Does an average-sized restaurant that sells two hundred pounds of chicken per week want to spend 500 dollars? Or would it prefer to spend 100 dollars? Which option do you suppose the chain restaurants choose?

The truth is, however, that there's more than money at stake. Large-scale manufacturers produce food behind closed doors. They don't want the public or the media to see how they transform raw ingredients into "food" wrapped in colorful packages and plastered with enticing slogans. As food ecologist Michael Pollan notes, the raw ingredients are processed into something that resembles their original state. But why won't they let anyone see how that food is prepared? The situation is different at Griggstown Farm and Market. Here, you can see the birds strutting their stuff every day. You can watch them run around, eat, and drink. These are healthy animals, humanely raised, free of the antibiotics, hormones, and chemicals that you inevitably ingest when you eat mass-produced, engineered, processed food. George has nothing to hide.

Slow Food can't succeed without farmers and supporters like George Rude. He does the work without seeking accolades, managing to keep the philosophy of

The market at Griggstown Quail Farm

Photo by Matt Sytsema

natural food and sustainability alive while going toe to toe with the mass producers. Because I know how tough it is to run a restaurant, I admire his ability to be both a hard-headed businessman and an advocate for genuine homegrown food. So the next time you start planning a family feast, I hope you'll give a thought to farmers like George. Every time you absentmindedly toss a White into your shopping cart, remember that you're essentially voting for a system that offers a mass-produced, unsustainable product that does more harm than good to the environment. Instead, seek out a local farm or a market that sells products from local farms. Give them your business, and your thanks. But if your local farm happens to be Griggstown, don't expect your gratitude will necessarily soften up George. More than once, people have told him that he's a hero of the Slow Food movement. To that, he growls: "Hey, Bud, ever heard of doing something just 'cause it's the right thing to do?"

✺

Following are a couple of chicken recipes from Tre Piani.

· · ·

Griggstown Farm Chicken with Apple Cider Glaze and Home-Fried Potatoes

Serves 2

FOR THE CHICKEN:

1 whole chicken breast, boned but
    with the skin on
Sea salt
Freshly ground black pepper
Extra-virgin olive oil
1 chopped shallot
1 cup apple cider
2 tbsp. brown sugar
1 sprig rosemary, stem removed,
    leaves finely chopped
2 leaves sage, finely chopped
2 tbsp. butter

FOR THE POTATOES:

1 pound local, freshly dug russet potatoes,
    peeled and cubed
¼ cup extra-virgin olive oil
1 onion, sliced
1 clove garlic, finely chopped
1 tsp. fresh thyme, finely chopped
Sea salt
Freshly ground black pepper
¼ tsp. cayenne

FOR THE CHICKEN: Season the chicken breast with salt and pepper. Over a medium flame, heat the olive oil in a large skillet. Sear the chicken skin side down until brown, then turn and brown the other side. Remove the breast from the pan and put it into an oven-proof dish. In a preheated 350-degree oven, bake the breast until done, about 10 minutes.

Meanwhile, add the chopped shallot to the skillet and cook at low heat until soft. Deglaze the skillet with the apple cider, add the brown sugar, and cook until the juices have reduced by two-thirds and become syrupy. Add the chopped herbs and salt and pepper to taste, and stir in the butter. Just before serving, pour the sauce over the chicken.

FOR THE POTATOES: Boil the potatoes in lightly salted water until tender and drain well. Heat the olive oil until very hot but not smoking in a large, heavy skillet. Season the potatoes with salt and pepper, and add them to the hot oil. Cook for about 10 minutes, turning them a couple times during the process. When the potatoes are brown, add the onions and garlic and cook until soft, about 5 more minutes. Season with thyme, salt, pepper, and cayenne.

Galantine of Griggstown Farm Chicken
and Micro–Beet Green Salad

Serves 8 as a light meal

FOR THE GALANTINE:
1 whole chicken
1 cup white wine
1 shallot, peeled and chopped
2 tbsp. fresh tarragon, finely chopped
Sea salt
Freshly ground white pepper
2 cups fresh spinach, washed and roughly chopped
¼ cup fresh morel mushrooms, roughly chopped (optional)
¼ cup sun-dried tomatoes, roughly chopped
½ cup hazelnuts, toasted and roughly chopped

FOR THE POACHING LIQUID:
3 cups chicken stock or broth
1 leek, split in half long-ways
2 bay leaves
2 cloves

FOR THE SALAD:
1 tbsp. whole-grain mustard
2 tbsp. sherry vinegar
¼ cup extra-virgin olive oil
Sea salt
Freshly ground black pepper
6 oz. micro–beet greens or other baby greens

FOR THE GALANTINE: Carefully remove the skin from the chicken in one piece: first, by cutting along the backbone, then by running your fingers between the skin and the meat. You will need to use a smaller knife to cut through the wing and leg areas. You should end up with a large piece of chicken skin. Set it aside.

Remove the breast meat in one piece and set it aside. Then remove the rest of the meat and set it aside separately. (Save the bones for stock. You can even use the stock as the base for the poaching liquid in this recipe.) Slice the breast meat into thin scaloppini. Refrigerate all meat parts until needed.

In a small pan, combine the wine, shallot, and tarragon and cook them together over medium heat until almost all the wine has evaporated. Now remove the loose, unsliced chicken meat from the refrigerator. Place in the bowl of a food processor and pulse until ground. Add the shallot and tarragon reduction and season with salt and pepper. Pulse again until well mixed. Remove the contents to a large bowl. Add the spinach, mushrooms, tomatoes, and hazelnuts, and mix well.

Remove the scaloppini and the reserved chicken skin from the refrigerator. On your counter, lay out a large piece of cheesecloth and, on top of it, the chicken skin, outside down. Place the slices of chicken breast in a single layer, leaving a I-inch space around the edges. Using a rubber spatula, spread the ground chicken and vegetable mixture onto the chicken breast in an even layer about ½-inch thick.

Carefully roll up the chicken skin around the filling, and then roll the cheesecloth around the chicken skin to form a large cylinder. Tie the roll on each end and in several places along the length, not too tightly. Refrigerate for at least an hour.

FOR THE POACHING LIQUID: Place the stock and seasonings into a pot wide enough to hold the roll and bring them to a simmer. Add the chicken roll and poach over low heat for about 30 minutes. Drain the roll and refrigerate it for at least 4 hours or overnight. (Keep the stock for another use.) When ready to serve, remove the string and cheesecloth from the chicken roll. Cut into ¼-inch slices and arrange on a platter.

FOR THE SALAD: In a large bowl, whisk together the mustard, vinegar, olive oil, and seasonings. Add the beet greens and toss. Arrange the salad over the chicken slices and serve.

ૐ   RESOURCES

Griggstown products can be found in many fine restaurants, food stores, and farmers' markets in the tri-state area.

Griggstown Quail Farm and Market
986 Canal Road
Princeton, NJ 08540
(908) 359–5218
http://www.griggstownquailfarm.com

For retail and wholesale purchases, you can also contact D'Artagnan in Jersey City:

D'Artagnan
(800) 327–8246
http://www.dartagnan.com

6

The Hat Lady

Pegi Ballister-Howells likes to say she wears forty-seven hats at once. Fortunately for the Slow Food movement, each of her hats represents her dedication to bringing good, clean, fair food from farm to table. And it doesn't hurt that she brings the talents of forty-seven people along with her.

Pegi has been essential to keeping the Slow Food philosophy alive and thriving, while also proving that people don't necessarily have to be card-carrying members of the movement to take part. "Slow Food isn't something you have to join with a banner—it needs to be how people *live*," she says. "If Slow Food can be a vehicle to get that message across, that's a gift. But the gift is a better quality of life. People need to understand that family dinners are critical, and kids need to know that fresh food is good. People need to know it's no harder to cook fresh broccoli than frozen broccoli. How hard is it to cook a beet? It's *not* hard! People need to make this part of their daily life. It's unfortunate we've gotten so far from the benefits of healthy food. We need Slow Food to remind us."

Pegi was an original co-leader and founding member of Slow Food Central New Jersey, and our chapter would not have been so successful without her insight and dedication. Today, though she is no longer a formal part of the movement, Pegi is still connected to all the critical elements that make Slow Food work. She's keyed in to the local farmers' point of view, and she also understands the viewpoint of the chefs and restaurant owners who want to purchase directly from those farmers rather than from a vast and anonymous mass food industry.

For fifteen years, Pegi was a marketing consultant at the New Jersey Farm Bureau, the liaison organization between agricultural producers and state government, so she is familiar with how state rules and regulations fit into food production and distribution. She also understands the indispensable role that Rutgers University has played in food research and education, both of which have been critical in bringing the Slow Food philosophy into the real world. Plus, Pegi is a communicator. Not only is she a writer, but she's also the host of popular food and gardening programs on radio and television, and she manages the website of the New Jersey Vegetable Growers Association. With years of marketing experience behind her, she is a primary influence in helping the many elements of the Garden State food world communicate with each other.

Pegi and I met in about 1999, just when Slow Food was getting started. She was already a well-known name in New Jersey food and gardening circles and a familiar presence on radio and TV. Her quirky, creative personality attracts and surprises people. They never quite know what she's going to do next. Who else could start out as a fashion designer at age eighteen and then go on to become a county extension agent?

During our first few Slow Food festivals, Pegi offered seminars about the food we were featuring—say, tomatoes, corn, or mushrooms—and she could talk for hours about almost anything that grows in the ground. Thinking back to those early days, she recently told me, "I remember when we made peach and cranberry sangria. Man, was that good!" Clearly, she appreciates the Slow Food focus on conviviality and hospitality; and as both a restaurant patron and a personal friend, she's been a joy and a gift.

Field of Dreams

I met Kim, my bride-to-be, one evening in Princeton, on my birthday. She was a recent arrival in town and thought that what the area really needed was a wine bar. Although she had no professional food or beverage experience, she was well traveled and, as I soon discovered, had impeccable taste and an incredible palate. Of course, I fell in love! After we decided to get married, we began planning the ceremony and reception, which we would hold at Tre Piani. By that time we had already begun construction on the Tre Bar, a wine bar with a small plate menu and Kim's original dream.

Months before the September 2006 event, Pegi began working on her wedding present to us. On Tre Piani's patio area, she planted a beautiful "field" of waving corn. Eventually the stalks grew so high you couldn't see through them. Around them were purple verbena and yellow marigolds. All summer people stopped, stared, and touched, asking, "Is that really corn?" Pegi was ecstatic. "It was stunning!" she remembers. "By September, the corn was at its prime, nice and tall. . . . Jim wanted a New Jersey fresh-food wedding, and this was perfect."

Tri-County Co-op auctioneer
Photo by Pegi Ballister-Howells

I think Pegi's wedding gift is an example of how people who really care about food and its nurture are interconnected. Whether you're a family sitting around the dinner table together or a tomato expert at Rutgers, you instinctively recognize how food helps make people happy. So when Pegi's tenth wedding anniversary rolled around, and she and her husband Tom made Tre Piani their first stop on their getaway weekend, you can be sure that we prepared a full-course menu of local foods to celebrate.

The Business Side of Slow Food

If Slow Food is to succeed long term, the concept needs to link to a solid distribution network from farm to table. Pegi is helping to do this through her work as manager of the Tri-County Cooperative Auction Market in East Windsor. Known locally as the Hightstown auction, it has been in existence since 1934 and has endured its share of slumps. When supermarkets began to thrive and food distribution became a huge automated process, small growers and farmers who relied on the co-op and the auction process were muscled out. But today the auction is seeing a comeback. Farmers, chefs, and the general public have become more aware of the benefits of buying and selling local food locally, and there is no doubt that Slow Food has helped to teach them about those benefits.

For 150 dollars a year, food producers—farmers, arborists, herb growers, vegetable gardeners, you name it—can become co-op members and sell their food or produce at the Hightstown auction. Still, even with more producers on board, there have been problems, many of them stemming from the auction's bidding hours, which traditionally opened at 7 P.M. As Pegi explained, "one of the big stumbling blocks between production and table is getting it from one place to the other. Evening hours were a serious problem. Nobody wanted to spend all night at the auction."

Yet the evening hours suited the producers, who then had the daylight hours to harvest and process their goods. So Pegi came up with a new idea: what if chefs and restaurant owners could order the food ahead of time directly from the farmer? Then, when they arrived at the auction, their order would be ready, and they could pick it up and leave immediately. Unfortunately, many farmers tend to resist change, and Pegi's idea looked like it might stall out. "Then, in the second year," she said, "an excellent grower from South Jersey discovered he could take orders ahead and have pallets of produce ready to go so that buyers could come into the auction, and grab the stuff, pay up, and leave. The plan did so well that other farmers started to copy it."

Today, the direct method amounts to 80 percent of the co-op's total sales, outselling traditional auction sales. And as Pegi pointed out, the new procedure "absolutely taps into the concept of Slow Food." The vast majority of the food available at the facility is freshly picked, in-season, local products. Even more innovations are on the way: the co-op recently received a grant to install a state-of-the-art cooler for storing fresh food so restaurant owners will have still more latitude about pickup times, and soon the co-op will also have a delivery truck.

Another success has been the co-op's community-supported agriculture (CSA) project, which allows the public into the co-op network. CSAs are springing up across the country, and they are a great way to acquire fresh, in-season, local food at bargain prices. For five hundred dollars, a family or an individual can join the co-op's CSA, a fee that entitles them to a crate of fresh, straight-from-the-farm produce every week for twenty weeks. The success of the program has been startling: in 2009–10, it contributed to a 62 percent increase in co-op sales, which now total more than 1 million dollars.

Farmers and the University

Pegi understands the farmers' side of things too. She's their liaison with the thicket of regulatory agencies, licensing bureaus, and whatnot that have become a major aspect of food production, distribution, and research. She also helps them with promotion and marketing, which are the parts of farming that farmers generally don't like. "Farmers like being their own boss, but they're not necessarily the best communicators, and they don't embrace change very quickly," Pegi said. "But physically, they can do anything. They are amazing! They can work all day long on a tractor and in the field, where tomato plants don't talk much. So it's not a natural transition to move from production to marketing, even though they recognize the need for it and appreciate efforts on their behalf."

So Pegi steps in to help. "Farmers are very busy, and marketing and promotion are not their strong suit, so they're glad somebody else is doing it. But they need to be very good producers—and if they can't sell it, there's no point in growing it. Plus, they need to pay even more attention to the rules and regulations, which have become more complicated . . . so the whole marketing and promotion thing becomes never-ending and takes more and more time."

On the other hand, farmers are the food chain's life blood. "Maybe it sounds cocky, but New Jersey farmers produce some of the finest fruits and vegetables in the world—we're not called the Garden State for nothing," Pegi told me. "We have excellent soils for growing, but land values are extraordinarily high, so in order to make a living as a farmer, you need to produce excellent quality in significant volume. To be a farmer here, you've got to be good. Then there are the ongoing educational requirements: for example, the kind you need in order to apply pesticides. And if you want to be an organic farmer today, there are all kinds of other regulations."

So it's not surprising that many of today's farmers seek out good educations and that many have graduated with science degrees. Pegi herself has degrees in biology and horticulture from Rutgers University, and she appreciates what Rutgers is doing to keep the "garden" in the Garden State. "Rutgers is the main event!" she said. She explained why its agricultural experiment station, the site of decades of cutting-edge research, has been indispensable to the New Jersey food industry: "Rutgers provides so many components for making the food industry viable." She noted that all of the state's county extension agents are Rutgers faculty members and that the university is involved in all aspects of coordinating educational requirements, credits, and licensing for growers and producers.

But research extends far beyond managing a bureaucracy. "Among the reasons that New Jersey is top of the line in agricultural production," Pegi said, "is the fact that Rutgers research is constantly dealing with issues as they come up, like putting out fires when diseases and new insects surface. Then there's the cutting-edge research into new varieties, into what's new and good, the best new crops for the future, what's the better tomato, the sweeter sweet corn? Those are all critical components. . . . Rutgers is always looking to the future—and it's helping to make New Jersey farmers among the best in the world!"

Planting the Seeds of Slow Food

How did Pegi get so good at understanding agriculture and the food industry while developing an instinctive feel for the Slow Food philosophy? The answer is that her own childhood was a Slow Food primer. Pegi grew up in the late 1950s in a huge Italian family. She was the youngest of eight kids, and appreciation of food was central to the family's everyday life. Although her father was a produce buyer, the family lived in gritty, urban northern New Jersey. Yet when her dad came home every night, he brought with him produce from all over the world, everything from mangoes to pomegranates. So Pegi really learned to appreciate food, even though "we never grew anything ourselves. What was the point?"

This was years before the Slow Food movement began, yet the family's approach to food had all of the movement's hallmarks. As Pegi said, "my father may not have known about the Slow Food concept, but he lived it, and I'm absolutely certain he would have embraced it." Under his influence, every food in the family's household was fresh. "My father never allowed frozen food in the house, and he *abhorred* fast-food joints. So every night, we had a bowl of greens, vegetables, potatoes, meat, salad, with all the kids at the table, and none of us were allowed to get up from the table until after Father had his coffee. . . . It was like the Slow Food movement every night!"

To this day Pegi won't buy frozen vegetables, though she does freeze and can her own fresh products. A lot of her cooking confidence comes from the fact that her mother set her loose in the kitchen when she was only nine years old. She proceeded to set the string beans on fire three times, and now she cracks, "I literally learned how to cook by fire."

Despite her early food experience, Pegi did not head straight into a food career when she grew up. While still in high school she became a professional tailor, and then she went to Boston to study fashion. By age eighteen, she had launched her own fashion line. But Pegi was restless, and before long "I fell in love with plants. I couldn't get enough of them, maybe because we never had a garden." So she went to Rutgers University and earned a bachelor's degree in biology, followed by a master's degree in horticulture. Her early years at home, plus her new career path, were starting to come together. "Who knew?" she laughed. "As soon as I got out of school and started to work for the county extension, I realized I had absorbed more about marketing produce than I had ever thought possible!"

Fortunately, Pegi had many chances to talk with her father about her goals, plans, and successes. Before he passed away in the late 2000s at the age of ninety-seven, "I told him I had started managing the Tri-County Auction, and he told me he used to come to the Tri-County Auction to buy produce. I had no idea. . . . Now I was in a position where my father's knowledge was unbelievably helpful. He had bought from wholesale vendors for sixty years, and he was a recognized force as a buyer. He knew how to handle problems with buyers, if anybody did, and he was the equivalent of my bigger buyers." She smiled. "He told me, 'Watch those auction guys, 'cause they are tough!'" Today, as an "auction guy" herself, Pegi just has to laugh.

ॐ

Following are a couple of Tre Piani recipes that use fresh New Jersey produce and other products available at the Tri-County Cooperative Auction Market.

- - -

Cranberry Sangria

Serves 4

½ cup sugar
½ cup local honey
Peel of 1 orange
1 cup water
1 pint dry-harvested New Jersey cranberries
    (American Cranberry Company is a good source)
1 bottle dry Riesling or other dry white wine
    (Unionville Vineyards in Ringoes, New Jersey, makes a good Riesling)

Boil the sugar, honey, orange peel, and water in a nonreactive saucepan for 2 minutes. Add the cranberries, and return to a boil. Lower heat and simmer until the berries are soft, about 1 minute. Let mixture cool, and add the wine.

Roasted Eggplant Salad

Serves 4

½ cup locally grown peppers, roasted, peeled, and cut into large dice
 (roasting instructions follow)
1 locally grown eggplant, peeled and cut into large dice
1 locally grown tomato, cut into large dice
8 oz. locally made fresh mozzarella, cut into large dice
3 leaves fresh basil, julienne cut
1 tbsp. balsamic vinegar
½ cup extra-virgin olive oil
Sea salt
Freshly cracked black pepper

TO ROAST THE PEPPERS: To roast peppers, you need to expose them to an extremely hot direct flame. The whole raw peppers can be cooked right on the grates of a barbecue grill, under a broiler, or even on the grates of the gas burner of your home stove. Large, thick-skinned, sweet varieties work best. Let the peppers cook until their skins are black and blistered and have started to loosen from the flesh. Turn them frequently. Once they are fairly evenly blackened all over, remove them from the fire, cover them, and let them steam in their remaining heat as they cool. After they have cooled, you can easily peel them. They will hold up in the refrigerator for a few days—even longer covered if they're covered with good olive oil.

TO MAKE THE SALAD: Preheat the oven to 400 degrees. In an oven-proof dish, toss the eggplant in ¼ cup of olive oil. Lightly salt and bake for 30 minutes, or until the eggplant is just cooked through. Let cool to room temperature.

Just before serving, transfer the eggplant to a large bowl and toss it with all of the remaining ingredients. If you like, you can mold the salad for presentation in a small bowl.

ᔇ RESOURCES

Tri-County Cooperative Auction Market
    http://www.tricountycoop.net

New Jersey Beekeepers Association
    http://www.njbeekeepers.org

American Cranberry Company
    http://www.americran.com

Unionville Vineyards
    http://www.unionvillevineyards.com

7

Getting the Word Out

Pat Tanner likes to tell the story of when she and I met. A food writer with a huge following, Pat came to Tre Piani in the late 1990s to interview me for one of her food columns. "A young chef making waves" is how she kindly explained her visit. But later that night she told her husband, Bill, what she really thought of me. "He's a nice guy," Pat said, "but I don't think we really connected." She was wrong, however. Pat and I became fast friends and for nine years were co-leaders of Slow Food Central New Jersey.

From the beginning, I was determined to get Pat interested in the Slow Food movement—and not just because she is a top-notch food critic and restaurant reviewer. Plenty of critics have good reputations but often because they are flashy with words rather than culinary experts. I have always wondered who was reviewing the reviewers: as far as I can tell most of them can't tell the difference between a soup and a sauce. No, I wanted Pat's support because she is a serious food advocate who understands what it takes to bring high-quality food to the table. Her professional life began when she opened her own catering business and cooked the food for it, which not all food-business owners do. With that real-world experience behind her, she has gone on to write a newspaper food column, host a radio show, and become a lively presence on the web. She also leads seminars, gives talks, and makes frequent public appearances.

When I decided to found a Slow Food chapter in central New Jersey, I knew that I needed to get the support of food pros: restaurant owners, farmers, small producers, and so on. But the movement also had to inspire the public. Otherwise, who would buy into the concept? Chapter organizers had to communicate the value of Slow Food to everybody, no matter who they were or where they were coming from. Who could do this? Pat Tanner. "When it came to developing our chapter and spreading the word on Slow Food, I saw my role as publicist," Pat recalled. She lined up cookbook authors for our annual Food & Wine festivals and organized dinners and speakers at ethnic restaurants that featured Peruvian, Ethiopian, Bulgarian,

Turkish, and many other cuisines. She wrote welcome letters to new members. Most important, she got the media interested in us and our Slow Food activities.

Pat stepped down as a chapter leader in 2009, yet she remains committed to the Slow Food movement. Our success proves, she believes, that great things can be accomplished in "tiny microscopic steps." For instance, "the fact that Michelle Obama has planted an organic garden on the White House lawn—if you would have told me in 1999 that such a thing could have happened in a twelve-year span, I would have said, 'No way!'"

Getting the Non-Joiner to Join

It was a coup to get Pat onto our Slow Food boat because she usually resists signing anybody's roster. "I don't join organizations of any kind," she said. "But remember, back then, Slow Food's slogan was 'Defending the pleasures of the table.'" As a food advocate, she saw that goal as worthy of support. We organizers had come together from all professional corners. What we had in common was that we all believed that our culture's infatuation with overprocessed, mass-produced food had gone far enough. It was time to remind people that another, better way was possible. Our palates were being robbed of "the pleasures of the table," and we needed to return to supporting local producers who provided us with high-quality, seasonal food.

Pat has always seen Slow Food as more than a movement or a philosophical statement about food. She sees it as a foundational idea, one that used to reflect how most people lived. "Every immigrant group that came to the United States found ways to take what they had grown up with in the homeland and managed to cobble together whatever was at hand." People brought with them traditions about preparing wholesome meals and assumed that good food should be available to everybody, even if it was not necessarily abundant. People were thoughtful and thrifty. They didn't waste, but most of them didn't want either. They knew who was producing and selling the food. They shopped at local mom-and-pop bodegas, bakeries, butcher shops, and fish markets and brought everything back to the family kitchen.

A Slow Food Upbringing

Pat was one of seven kids in the Liuzza family, a hardworking Italian clan that settled in urban northern New Jersey. Her father was a factory worker, her mother

A food-drive stand at the winter farmers' market at Tre Piani

Photo by Jim Weaver

an accomplished homemaker who turned out satisfying and creative meals—though back then *creative* simply meant doing what you could with what you had. I, too, find that some of my best recipes were inspired from necessity rather than my own creativity. Some people might say that sensibility is reflected in today's popular Food Network challenges in which contestants have to cook something memorable from underwhelming ingredients. But the point isn't to celebrate the idea of poverty. No, Pat's family instinctively understood what Slow Food calls "conscious eating." That means being aware of what you put in your bodies and using the food you have at hand, wisely and well.

Pat recalled, "We managed to cobble together whatever was at hand. My Italian grandmother could not afford to buy meat in the United States, so she started making red sauce with pork neck bones. There was some marrow in the bone, so it gave the dish a wonderful, rich taste of pork." As a child, she went with her mother to butcher shops that were still so Old World that their floors were strewn with sawdust. (This remains a surprisingly effective way of controlling odor and cleanliness when animal products are involved.) Wherever they shopped, the point was to select the best food, frugally and wisely. From those early excursions with her mother, Pat learned that sometimes the most delicious fish are the cheapest—for instance, fresh sardines. She remembered coming home with a haul of fresh clams in net bags, which would be transformed into huge platters of clams with linguini: "It was all wonderfully flavorful, wholesome food."

Yet even though Pat had been skilled in the kitchen since childhood, cooking didn't seem like a career. Instead, she became a corporate trainer for a management development firm. But she was constantly traveling and felt as if her two daughters were growing up without her. "I thought, 'How can I control my own hours, doing something I love?'" The answer was right under her nose: food. Soon she was cooking and catering out of a rented kitchen at the local Elks Club. (New Jersey state regulations don't allow commercial cooking in a private home.) But as her business took off, Pat found she had less family time than ever.

Then one day, she heard that a slot had suddenly opened up at the local newspaper for someone to write a recipe column. The new lifestyle editor had thought of Pat. "Well, I knew I could cook, but I had never written a journalistic word in my life," Pat told me. That night, however, she went home, took out a legal pad, and challenged herself to see how many ideas for food columns she could set down. "Within twenty minutes, I had filled over two pages," she laughed. "Hmm . . . maybe I can do this!"

Rounding Up the Farmers

In Slow Food Central New Jersey's crucial startup years, organizers saw one task as most important: to get local farmers and local restaurants to connect and work together. One of our first opportunities came at Har-Fest, which I've mentioned in chapter 1. It was a sumptuous combination of banquet and food fair featuring menu items and wines from restaurants and producers all over the area. As we chefs and cooks served up our bounty, the farmers stood alongside us. The public could ask them questions about the actual plot of land which had produced the ear of corn or the tomatoes on their plate. As Pat recalled, "It doesn't sound earth-shattering anymore, but back then, it was a totally novel idea. Nobody was doing it."

"Of all the groups I've dealt with, I love the farmers the best," Pat said. "They are the most genuine. They love this land, this Garden State, and oftentimes they are the sixth or seventh generation working the family farm. What they find difficult is having to market themselves. It's something totally foreign to them: some of them have only worked wholesale markets and auctions, and they aren't even used to dealing with retailers, let alone the actual consumer. So a lot of them don't enjoy it. But others just take to it, and they love interacting."

Pat understood the power of having farmers and the public interact because she had seen it happen in her own life. "Remember, I was raised in northern New Jersey; it couldn't have been a more urban environment. But when I was raising my two daughters, I lived for ten years in tract housing in East Windsor. Our backyard opened up onto the Lee Turkey Farm. There wasn't even a fence between us. Our girls watched the corn rise up taller than they were, and they could wake up in the morning and smell the strawberries growing in the fields. So I had grown to know and love what the agricultural side of our state was and could be." It was painful for her to see that so many other neighbors never made that connection: "It was as if a complete wall existed between their homes and the farm. They never visited the farm or bought a turkey there. So I took on the Slow Food movement for that reason. I wanted to share what I knew. I wanted to say, 'Look what's there, right in your backyard!'"

At the Table, All Are Equal

The Slow Food movement gathered steam because we had such a great variety of people involved. We were truly a diverse band: restaurant owners and chefs, wholesalers and retailers, family farmers and small greengrocers. Rutgers University research was enabling us to rescue and restore foods that were being neglected and endangered because they didn't fit into the paradigm of the mass food industry. We were becoming a whole community, and in community lies power. "The connection among us was incredible," Pat said. "All these highly motivated individuals coming from such different perspectives; it was a really good combination of skills and motivations. As a food writer and reviewer, I couldn't be more excited. I wanted the whole world to know about it."

To promote conviviality and hospitality is one of the pillars of Slow Food, and that's been the subject of several of Pat's interviews and food articles—including one about me. A few years ago a reporter from the *Montclair Times* asked her, "Who's the most intimidating person you've ever cooked for?" Pat's answer: Jim Weaver. Her tale took place on Thanksgiving, the year we'd founded our Slow Food chapter, and Pat was making her usual bountiful feast. Pat recalled, "Jim had become such a good friend. He works all those countless hours, cooking for all those benefits, and I'm famous for my wonderful Thanksgiving dinners; so I said, 'Give yourself a break. Come to my house for dinner.'" Yet immediately Pat began

Pat Tanner and Chef Emeril Lagasse

Photo by Bill Tanner

experiencing host remorse: "What was I thinking! He's the most talented chef I know! Well, okay, he's the least judgmental person, too, and, okay, I'm not cooking Italian that night, right?"

Her turkey was wonderful. But to this day, perfectionist Pat will tell you she thinks it was exceptionally dry that year and that the whole evening "was the worst Thanksgiving meal I ever made. I think I was way too self-conscious." Of course she's wrong (though to get a food critic to admit to any shortcoming should be music to a chef's ears). But she and I also share another memory, this one about a later meal we had together: the presence, center table, of one of George Rude's exquisite turkeys, a Bourbon Red, one of about eight in the classic line of Heritage Breeds that I introduced you to in chapter 5. "In the early days George knew he would not make money on the Heritage Breed turkey, that it was a losing proposition," Pat remembered. "But he agreed to raise them as a favor to us, and now they are a tremendous success, and George sells out of them every year."

When we first ate a holiday dinner together, the Heritage Breed turkeys were not available. But now they are, and Pat never has to worry about serving a boring bird again. Yet mistakes happen: one year the shop happened to give her the wrong bird. When she opened up the carton at home, there lay a flabby Broad-Breasted White. Pat panicked; what would Thanksgiving be without one of George Rude's Heritage Breed turkeys? The shop quickly rectified the mistake, but the snafu was a classic example of how Slow Food has reawakened America's palates. Once you taste a classic, you can't go back.

ॐ

Following are a few of Pat Tanner's kitchen specialties.

Cranberry-Pear Relish

Makes about 3 cups

1¼ cups sugar
I cup water
¼ cup lemon juice, plus extra if desired
1½ pounds firm local pears, peeled, cored, and chopped coarsely
3 cups local cranberries, rinsed and picked over
1¼ tsp. lemon zest
¼ tsp. ground cinnamon
¼ tsp. ground allspice

In a stainless steel or enameled saucepan combine sugar, water, and ¼ cup lemon juice and bring to a boil, stirring, until the sugar is dissolved. Simmer the mixture for 5 minutes. Add pears and cranberries, return mixture to a boil, and simmer for 5 to 7 minutes or until the cranberries pop and the mixture thickens.

Remove pan from the heat and stir in lemon zest, cinnamon, and allspice. Let the relish cool and add more lemon juice to taste, if desired. Transfer the relish to a ceramic or glass bowl and chill it, covered, overnight. It keeps, covered and chilled, for about a week.

Deviled Quail Eggs with Truffle Butter

Serves 6 as an appetizer, more if you pass them as snacks at a cocktail party

24 quail eggs
Truffle butter, softened (available from D'Artagnan)
Whole-fat mayonnaise
Salt, preferably coarse Sicilian sea salt
Freshly cracked black pepper

Place quail eggs in a pan and cover with at least 1 inch of cold water. Bring to a slow boil over medium heat and cook gently for 5 minutes. Run under cold water; crack and peel. (This is tedious work, but you'll get faster at it over time.)

Cut each egg in half horizontally and place yolks in a small bowl. Add truffle butter and mayo to taste at a ratio of about twice as much butter to mayo; combine well. Continue adding butter and mayo until the mixture reaches a light, airy consistency. Add salt and pepper to taste.

Fill each egg white half with the yolk mixture, using either a pastry bag without a tip (the truffle bits get stuck in even the largest tip) or a demitasse spoon. Eggs will keep overnight, covered and refrigerated.

Potato-Turnip Bake

Makes 2 quarts

According to Pat, "other than to remember that I pulled the original version from a so-called ladies' magazine in the early 1980s, I can only say that the provenance of this recipe is lost in time. But for decades now my family insists that it is not Thanksgiving without it. One of its best features is that it's assembled a day in advance. I have to admit I never cook it the same way twice. If the potatoes are on the soft side and the turnips a bit hard, I have been known to cook them together for the same length of time."

6 large locally grown russet potatoes, peeled and cut into chunks
3 large locally grown turnips, peeled and cut into chunks
½ cup finely chopped, locally grown onion
¼ cup unsalted butter
3 tbsp. finely chopped parsley
Sea salt
Freshly ground black pepper
¾ cup shredded cheddar

In a big pot, cover potatoes with cold water by at least an inch and add a pinch of salt. Bring to a boil, and cook for 10 minutes. Add turnips and onion, and cook for 15 more minutes or until the potatoes and turnips are soft. Drain and mash with the butter, parsley, and salt and pepper to taste.

Remove 1 cup of the mixture and place in a pastry bag with a large tip. Transfer the rest of the mixture to a 2-quart casserole and decoratively pipe the contents of the bag around the edge. Cover and chill for several hours or overnight. Bake, uncovered, in a preheated 350-degree oven for 35 to 40 minutes. Sprinkle the top with the cheddar and bake for an additional 5 minutes.

ᦟ **RESOURCES**

For truffle-based products as well as many specialty meats, check this website:

D'Artagnan
http://www.dartagnan.com

8

Triumph of the Locavores

To appreciate the Slow Food philosophy, you've got to start thinking outside the plastic fast-food box. Most people have become so conditioned to processed foods that it's hard for them to get past that comfort level. If you're trapped in a conventional way of thinking, it's easy to throw a chunk of emulsified cheese or packaged hamburger into the grocery cart or feel satisfied with an after-dinner verdict of "Well, that tasted pretty good." That status-quo attitude is hard to overcome. So the activists who are working to bring food back to a higher standard are some of the twenty-first century's true innovators, entrepreneurs, and risk takers. And among them stands Patrick Martins.

Patrick helped to found Slow Food USA, importing the concept from Italy, where he worked with Carlo Petrini, who had established the parent organization, Slow Food International, in the mid-1980s. But Patrick went beyond the idea of simply bringing the movement to America. He figured out how to translate it into practical reality. In other words, he answered the question: how do you get a sustainable local food supply from its source to America's dining tables? In 2001 Patrick established Heritage Foods USA, which began as the sales and marketing arm of Slow Food USA. It's the distribution network that moves fresh, sustainable local products from farms and local growers to restaurants, mom-and-pop stores, farmers' markets, and beyond. In 2004, Heritage Foods USA became an independent company and added another mission: to save many of the country's traditional livestock breeds, which are in danger of extinction.

The Food Fighter from Brooklyn

Patrick directs Heritage Foods USA from his Brooklyn apartment. I don't know quite how he does it, but the system works. In the process, he has become an icon for foodies everywhere. He's been featured in publications ranging from *Esquire* to the *New York Times Magazine,* which gave him the nickname "Food Fighter." But for all his celebrity, Patrick remains a real working guy. If you call his office, the assistant who answers the phone is liable to say, "He'll be with you shortly; he's hanging pork jowls at the moment."

To other people, Patrick can feel like a force of nature: you get swept up by his energy. That's what happened to me when I first contacted him. At the time he was living in Italy and working with Carlo Petrini. Introducing myself, I told him I was interested in developing our Slow Food chapter in New Jersey. A native New Yorker to the core, Patrick's immediate response was to hoot at the notion of linking Slow Food to New Jersey, which the Empire State thinks of as its poor cousin. But once he realized that New Jersey has long been the source and champion of farm-to-plate food, he changed his tune—especially once I sent him the press clippings about our popular Slow Food events. When he learned that membership in Slow Food Central New Jersey was at three hundred and growing, Patrick was flabbergasted. He said they would have to dedicate one of the drawers in the file cabinet in the Slow Food International office in Bra to our chapter.

After this first contact, we quickly went from being colleagues to friends. Over the phone, I had imagined a tall, wiry academic with glasses and short hair. In person, Patrick's rumpled and wild-eyed, like the kid from science class who enjoys explosions and computer games. But it's easy to see how I got the egghead idea: Patrick can riff for hours about sustainability, genetic diversity, and establishing a fully traceable food supply. He sees the Slow Food movement as a solidarity struggle. According to Patrick, when you agitate for something to exist that's outside the norm (in this case, authentic, fresh foods versus the processed, corporate variety), "that's a subversive act." He appreciates people who fight for those principles, and he thinks that's why he and I get along. "Jim has that activist gene in him," Patrick likes to say. "That's why we're connected spirits."

An Underground Railroad

When he came back from Italy, Patrick wanted to put our "connected spirits" to work. He had an idea; and when Patrick has an idea, brace for impact. He was starting up Heritage Foods USA and had his eye on delivering fresh, locally grown foods into the heart of Manhattan, where it would be available to the city's great restaurants as well as all around the tri-state area. But he needed a distribution center. "You know anybody who has a refrigerated warehouse who could take local meat shipments?" he asked. Well, Tre Piani has a very large walk-in refrigerator and has fairly easy access to a huge loading dock. And it's less than an hour from New York City. . . . So it began.

Today, Patrick compares those fledgling shipments from my Princeton walk-in into New York City with the beginnings of the underground railroad. The idea was so new that a route hadn't even been worked out. "We were so off the grid," Patrick likes to say, "we didn't even have a phone number yet!" Each Wednesday, a huge tractor trailer would show up loaded with boxes of meat packed by Paradise Locker in Missouri. All of it came from livestock that had been traditionally and humanely raised in the nation's heartland. The next day, Patrick would rumble into Princeton with his rented van, pick up the meat, and then return to Manhattan for a long day of deliveries. Those boxes went to restaurants headed by award-winning chefs such as Daniel Boulud, Mario Batali, and Mark Ladner, among other high-profile names. Batali, who has found fame on the Food Network and in countless cookbooks, says he won't use any pork unless it comes from Heritage Foods. Luckily, a few of the boxes also stayed with me. The meat they contained show-cased the great, traditionally raised animals that would have been delicious and familiar fare to Americans a century ago: Red Waddle pork loins, Thunder Heart bison, Katahdin lamb shanks. All of it was super-fresh. It looked better, smelled better, and had much better texture and flavor than typical boxed meats do.

As with all startups, however, there were glitches and adventures. The first time Patrick tried to get his meat-filled van through the Holland Tunnel, he was turned away because his truck was too big. So he had to regroup and race north over some of the country's heaviest traveled roadways to get to the Lincoln Tunnel, the only other way into New York City. This wouldn't have been a big deal, except that he was carrying refrigerated meats. But he was only a *little* late. Today, he gives credit to those famous chefs who cut him some slack and looked the other way as the Heritage operation got up to speed.

This Meat Cannot Be Beat

A great chef understands that in order to prepare truly good food, you need to begin with the best ingredients. The meats and other foods available through Heritage are great for several reasons, and there is a story behind them all. People who dine at world-class restaurants love having the opportunity to taste something that is truly wonderful or that takes them back to a flavor they remember from childhood. They want food that makes a lasting impression and gives them something to talk about.

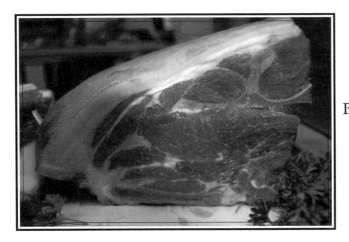

Berkshire pork shoulder

Photo by Jim Weaver

Take Thunder Heart bison, for example. Instead of processing hundreds of animals at a time, Thunder Heart Ranch in Texas raises free-ranging bison that roam at will, eating native grasses and plants. At slaughter, they are processed one at a time by a low-stress method. Afterward, workers hold a Native American–style ceremony for each animal before it is sent fresh to Heritage customers around the country. The meat, naturally low in fat, is deep red in color and has a sweet, full flavor. The texture is buttery with a slight crispness; and if you let a thin slice of the tenderloin sit on your tongue, it will almost melt like fine chocolate. You cannot find this quality at the supermarket.

Most beef available at standard markets and restaurants is what we commonly call "boxed beef," processed from animals that have spent their lives in disgusting and often cruel concentrated animal feeding operations (CAFOs) before going through the slaughterhouse, into cryo-vac plastic, and finally into an enormous cardboard box. These boxes, each of which can weigh as much as a hundred pounds, are shipped to distributors all over the country and beyond. The special shrink wrap known as cryo-vac eliminates oxygen and allows the meat to last in the refrigerator for many weeks without spoiling or freezing. (Freezing is probably the single worst thing that can be done to a piece of meat.) This preservation method is excellent for those who buy and sell large volumes of meat. But it is not the best way to ensure the quality of the meat, though unfortunately most people cannot taste the difference. There are even a couple of restaurant chains that call this method of storing meat "wet aging"—a boldfaced lie if you happen to know anything about meat.

It is true, however, that some of the best-tasting beef in the world is "dry aged." Fresh, unbagged meat with the bone in (usually short loin or shell steak) is aged in a special refrigerator for about three weeks, with strong fans and a black light to control mold. When the meat is ready, the entire outside and the bones are discarded, about 25 percent of the weight. What is left in the center is extraordinarily tender meat with a mildly musty odor that is desirable to steak connoisseurs. You can understand why it costs more than so-called wet-aged meat, which is simply pulled from a cryo-vac bag and cut, with zero effort or waste.

I am also a big fan of Heritage lamb. So much of the lamb that you see in American restaurants and markets comes frozen from New Zealand. When meat is frozen, the water inside the cells expands and bursts. Then, when the meat defrosts, the flavor in the juices runs out, and the meat is dry. I have always preferred the flavor of American lamb, and now I have a chance to cook rare breeds such as Romney and Katahdin that do not need much embellishment from me to taste great. I am always happy to have the food itself do my work!

Rooting for Our Heritage

Everybody from chefs, to foodies, to farmers, to every Slow Food supporter in the country was rooting for Patrick and Heritage Foods USA. Its success would transform the Slow Food movement from an abstract philosophy into a real-world force in the food industry. At the same time, Slow Food forces were gathering all around the United States, many behind longtime pioneers and inspirers of the idea. Among those pioneers is Alice Waters, chef, educator, author, a Slow Food USA vice president, and a founder of the movement. From her base in Berkeley, California, Alice has spent four decades promoting sustainable, locally grown agriculture. Her restaurant, Chez Panisse, is dedicated to using only the finest locally grown and raised foods. In 1996 she founded the Edible Schoolyard, a one-acre garden-classroom that trains students to think about food in eco-gastro-economic terms. Education is at the heart of the Slow Food philosophy, and Alice's innovations have forged the way.

Under the inspirational glow of Alice Waters and her work, Slow Food sensibilities were growing on the West Coast. In the mid-2000s, Jen Maiser, Jessica Prentice, Sage Van Wing, and DeDe Sampson coined the term *locavores* to describe foodies who believe in fueling the body with local food. The name caught fire like a match in a bowl of gasoline. It soon spread into the public consciousness via the *San Francisco Chronicle* and other media. Soon the four women, who called themselves "concerned culinary adventurers," were challenging Bay Area residents to spend one month eating only what was grown within a hundred-mile radius. The locavore campaign was irresistible and has become a tradition.

Authors and investigative writers also energized the movement. In particular, Michael Pollan raised public consciousness with his books *The Omnivore's Dilemma* and *Food Rules*. With stomach-churning precision, he spelled out exactly how far we've strayed from producing real food. In *The Omnivore's Dilemma*, for instance, he described the atrocious living conditions of modern cows, who lumber around on an artificially fattening diet of subsidized corn chased by cocktails of hormones and chemicals. Pollan compared the conditions in modern feedlots to concentration camps.

Meanwhile, higher education has also taken note of the Slow Food philosophy. Chapters have sprung up on many campuses, including Rutgers University. I've already discussed the New Jersey Agricultural Experiment Station's research into sustainable, local product development, but the university's commitment extends beyond scientific research and academic inquiry to programs such as the Rutgers Gardens Farmers Market and the Rutgers Food Innovation Center. These hands-on, brick-and-mortar entities bring the reality of sustainable food to students and consumers. Clearly, across the country, thousands of us are committed to bringing the Slow Food philosophy back to America's table. Yet as my own experiences prove, we face an uphill battle.

A Restaurant Owner's Dilemma

When I stock my kitchen at Tre Piani, I know I can't purchase everything locally. Many ingredients come from around the world, and are sold to me through a network of importers, distributors, and delivery companies. Climate and seasonal changes limit what we can produce in New Jersey, and the same is true in every state. My menu highlights local ingredients whenever possible. But I have to maintain a consistent style year round, in season or out.

And that's the rub. As most locavores and Slow Food devotees know, it's almost impossible to run a restaurant without shipping ingredients long distances. So we end up making a devil's bargain with the planet because we're forced to expend valuable transportation resources and leave behind a huge carbon footprint. But if I try to be a purist and limit my menu to only what is locally available, I'll go out of business. After all, you can't cook without oils, salt, pepper, spices, and vinegars. How about a restaurant without coffee and tea? Or how would you run a restaurant without wine and liquor? From chocolate to flour to condiments, many ingredients that are perceived as necessary are usually from out of state. And if they are produced in New Jersey, they may not be available in large-enough quantities to satisfy my business.

Likewise, New Jersey doesn't produce great amounts of beef, pork, lamb, or bison. I hate to say it, but restaurants are forced to purchase their meat prefabricated. In other words, I order only the parts I need. Very few restaurants can turn an entire 2,500-pound steer, hoof to ears, into a profitable food source by butchering it in their kitchens. Instead, we pick and choose. Fine-dining and upscale restaurants use the loin portions for filet mignon, New York strip, porterhouse, and rib-eye steaks. Everybody uses various other parts for sauces and stews. Although these "lesser" cuts are the makings for many of the world's best dishes, including ropa vieja and boeuf bourguignon, not to mention hamburgers, we just cannot manage 1,800 pounds of leftover skin, guts, and fat.

But our problems go beyond efficiency. Heritage Foods USA and the Slow Food movement are battling on a second front too: quality versus convenience. The problem is, the more we are conditioned for convenience, the more we seem to crave it. Sometimes, in my gloomier moments, I imagine a bleak world that resembles an updated version of *Animal Farm* or *1984* and where, every day, citizens troop obediently to the nearest fast-food outlet, queue up on a conveyor belt, open their mouths wide, and get fed squirts of the day's recommended allowance of nutrients. I wish my nightmare were more far-fetched than it really is. Because right now, in the real world, all across America, cars are lined up at fast-food drive-in windows, waiting to receive their orders of processed cattle parts and emulsified spices. I wonder what our hunting and gathering ancestors would think of that sight.

The "Turkey Cam" Rules

In mass-production food factories, outsiders are never allowed to see what goes on inside. The operation is riddled with security checkpoints, armed guards, electric fences, and cameras pointed at you, not at the animals. Try to guess which farm contributed the beef in your Big Mac. There's no way you'll ever know.

In contrast, take a look at Patrick's "turkey cam." Located on one of the turkey farms sponsored by Heritage Foods USA, it is aimed into the pens and shows what it records online, 24/7. The simple message is that the operation has nothing to hide. This kind of transparency is what has made Heritage Foods USA a success. Today, it serves 350 restaurants and is supported by fifty farms across the

Counter at Meat Hook in Brooklyn, which buys from Heritage Foods
Photo by Jim Weaver

United States. Meats and poultry are its cornerstones, but Heritage also offers seafood, cheeses, wild rice, honey, and more. Everything is naturally raised without antibiotics, artificial preservatives, or growth hormones, and each product can be traced to specific farms and actual people. Information about each source is highlighted on the Heritage website. Moreover, as I discussed in chapter 5, Heritage has undertaken a Rare Breeds Project. Though it began as campaign to save endangered turkeys, today it has expanded to include Native American foods, pigs, sheep, bison, cows, reef-net salmon, goats, as well as products such as honey and wild rice. The list is constantly growing.

So is Heritage Foods USA a success? Of course. Has it totally changed the way America eats? Well, not yet. But Patrick's genius is that he knows how to mix his activist fire with the art of compromise. On the one hand, his passion and enthusiasm have made great inroads in bringing sustainable agriculture and authentic, locally produced foods to restaurants and food lovers across America. Yet on the other hand, Patrick works doggedly, day by day, in pursuit of the smallest of incremental successes. He says, "People think they have to do something really significant to get something done—that it's all or nothing. But that's not true. If every corporate chef in America dedicated 5 percent of his purchases to sustainable and local foods, it could have an impact on tens of thousands of small farmers."

So chefs shouldn't get discouraged if just part of their menu is locally based. After all, Patrick didn't get discouraged because he could save only one turkey breed at a time, or could only sign up fifty farms rather than a hundred, or had to turn back from his first distribution run at the Holland Tunnel. Each Slow Food success, large or small, means something. As Patrick puts it, "If more people just did a little, it would work."

ॐ

Following are a couple of my own recipes using Heritage meat products. I've also included a recipe by Chef Michael Anthony of the famed Gramercy Tavern.

Slow-Roasted Berkshire Pork Shoulder

Enough for a crowd and then some

1 bone-in pork shoulder, about 6 pounds
3 tsp. crushed black peppercorns
¼ cup kosher salt
2 gallons extra-virgin olive oil
1 head garlic
2 tsp. whole fennel seeds
2 tsp. crushed juniper berries
4 bay leaves
Zest of 2 lemons

Rub pork all over with salt and pepper, and let it sit at room temperature for about 2 hours. Place pork, skin side up, in a heavy, high-sided roasting pan or pot, and add all of the remaining ingredients. Cover with aluminum foil and roast in a preheated 300-degree oven for at least 6 hours. Remove pan from oven, and let the roast cool in the oil for 30 minutes before transferring it to a carving board. Slice thin and serve warm.

The oil can be strained and kept in the refrigerator or a cool place for another use.

Pan-Seared Filet of Beef with Sliced Jersey Tomatoes, Marinated Portabella Mushrooms, and Blue Cheese

Serves 4

2 cloves garlic, sliced
½ cup extra-virgin olive oil
1 tsp. crushed red pepper
2 large portabella mushrooms, sliced into ½-inch pieces
1 tbsp. balsamic vinegar
1 tsp. chopped fresh parsley
¼ cup extra-virgin olive oil
4 6-ounce filet mignons, preferably from a grass-fed cow
2 Jersey tomatoes
¼ cup crumbled blue cheese, preferably local
Sea salt
Freshly ground black pepper

In a skillet over low heat, lightly brown the garlic in the olive oil. Add the red pepper, mushrooms, vinegar, and parsley. Season with salt and pepper, and set aside.

Heat a large sauté pan and add the oil. Season the filets with salt and pepper. Add the filets to the pan and cook over medium heat. They will need to cook about 4 minutes per side for medium rare.

Slice the tomatoes. Drain the reserved mushrooms, saving the liquid. Place two large slices of tomato and a filet on each plate. Divide the mushrooms into 4 equal portions and spread over the filet. Drizzle a little of the marinade over the beef and tomatoes. Sprinkle the entire plate with crumbled blue cheese.

Pasture-Raised Chicken with Pickled Ramps, Asparagus, and Spring Onions

Michael Anthony, Gramercy Tavern

Serves 4

BRINE FOR CHICKEN BREASTS:
1 gallon water
1 cup light-brown sugar, packed
1 cup granulated white sugar
2 cups salt
1 tbsp. mustard seed
2 tbsp. crushed black pepper
3 cloves garlic, crushed
3 sprigs thyme
1 bay leaf
1 cup white-wine vinegar

BRINED AND BAKED CHICKEN:
4 pasture-raised boneless chicken breasts
Sea salt
Freshly ground black pepper
2 tbsp. extra-virgin olive oil
4 sprigs thyme

PICKLED RAMPS:
3 cups granulated white sugar
3 cups water
9 cups rice-wine vinegar
½ cup sea salt
¼ tsp. mustard seed
¼ tsp. black peppercorns
¼ tsp. fennel seed
¼ tsp. coriander seed
1½ quarts ramps, trimmed

ASPARAGUS AND SPRING ONIONS:
20 spears asparagus
8 bulbs spring onions, white part only
1 tbsp. extra-virgin olive oil
Sea salt
Freshly ground black pepper

BRINE FOR CHICKEN BREASTS: Combine all ingredients and bring to a boil. Remove from heat and let cool.

BRINED AND BAKED CHICKEN: Submerge chicken breasts into the cooled brine, and refrigerate for 24 hours. Remove and pat dry before cooking.

Preheat oven to 400 degrees. Season breasts with salt and pepper. Heat a large, ovenproof skillet and add olive oil. Over medium heat, sear chicken on all sides until golden brown. Add thyme sprigs to pan. Place in oven and cook for 20 minutes more, turning chicken at least once. Remove from oven and set aside.

PICKLED RAMPS: Mix all ingredients except the ramps and bring to boil. Remove from heat and strain. Let cool. Add ramps. Chill. (Extra pickled ramps can be refrigerated and used in salads, soups, and sandwiches.)

ASPARAGUS AND SPRING ONIONS: Cut asparagus spears into 1-inch lengths. Blanch in boiling water for about 1 minute, and immediately submerge in ice water. Drain well when cool.

Slice spring onion bulbs into thin wedges. In a pan over medium heat, briefly cook the onions in olive oil until they are soft but not browned. Season with salt and pepper to taste.

TO ASSEMBLE THE DISH: Mix together the pickled ramps with the asparagus and spring onions. To serve, arrange the vegetables on a plate, and place the chicken breasts, skin side up, on top.

ᘐ RESOURCES

Heritage Foods USA is a great source for the meats in these recipes. The company can ship its products anywhere in the continental United States, either wholesale or retail. Most of the restaurants that use Heritage products are listed on the website.

Heritage Foods USA
   http://www.heritagefoodsusa.com

9

Salumeria Biellese

A definition of happiness: to be a restaurant owner with a space to fill. That's where my fiancée Kim and I found ourselves in 2006, about six months before our wedding, as we looked at the empty space we were already imagining as Tre Piani's small-plate and wine bar, Tre Bar. Our restaurant had already earned a reputation as a supporter of food that's "good, clean, and fair." Now our wine-bar menu had to reflect the same philosophy of authenticity and quality. Besides, if you don't have a clear idea of what you want to serve, you will probably end up with the wrong equipment and a space that doesn't work very efficiently. So we had a menu to script, and it was time to hit the road for some serious research.

We knew one of our must-haves was a great salumi selection. "Salumi?" you ask. "Aren't you spelling it wrong? You mean *salami*, right?" Actually, no. In the United States, we've come to call nearly every dried and salted meat *salami*, although that word really refers to a specific subgroup of cured meats that are usually made of beef or a beef-pork mix. The appropriate term for the complete family of cured-meat products is *salumi*; and in pursuit of it Kim and I made a thirty-five-mile hop into the heart of Manhattan to visit one of the oldest and greatest salumi businesses in New York, Salumeria Biellese.

In 1943 Ugo Buzzio assumed ownership of a small deli and salumeria on the corner of Eighth Avenue and Twenty-eighth Street. The roots of his business can be traced back to the small town of Curino, just outside Biella, an old textile town that lies at the foot of the Alps in northern Italy. Here Ugo learned the art of butchering and salumi making from Mario Fiorio. Working alongside him was Mario's son Piero; and when Ugo decided to move to New York, Piero soon followed. Eventually, Ugo, his son Marc Buzzio, Sergio Gabrielli, Piero Fiorio, and Ugo's son-in-law Paul Valetutti established the Salumeria Biellese, a deli, catering, and artisanal salumi shop. Today the company is owned and operated by Marc Buzzio, Paul Valetutti, and Paul's brother in-law, Fouad Alsharif. In the late 1980s, they also opened a restaurant: Biricchino, at 376 Eighth Avenue.

Salumeria Biellese in New York City

Photo by Jim Weaver

Both are located just a few blocks south of Penn Station and Madison Square Garden.

Salumi is meat that has been preserved with salt. You're probably familiar with many of the better-known salumi, such as the many varieties of ham, salami, pepperoni, and soppresatta. Like many time-honored food traditions, salumi making was born of necessity and then developed into an art form. Traditionally, it was a way to deal with a basic problem of meat raising: when you slaughter a pig, you're left with too much meat to eat at one time. As a way to preserve meat for consumption during the winter months, the process reaches back to ancient Rome. Not only did the Romans enjoyed eating dried meats, but they even wrote laws on how to regulate production. Today, from four-star restaurants to farmers' markets, supermarkets, agritourismos, and small family homes, southern Europe abounds with thousands of varieties of salumi.

Like great cheese, salumi is a natural pairing with wine. This trio goes together well for reasons that are both as obvious and as mysterious as nature itself. Each expresses the unique *terroir*, or taste of the place from where it came. That means that a salumi or a cheese from, say, Italy's Piedmont region will have the subtle characteristics of that soil and climate. What's more, each of these ancient foodstuffs owes its depth and personality to the natural artistry of time rather than to hyped-up production schedules and emulsifiers. Both wine and cheese are the natural outcome of fermentation, whereas salumi is the natural outcome of salt curing.

Kim and I have had great salumi all over southern Europe, where it is part of daily life for many people. We first tasted Iberico ham—the holy grail of ham—in the Las Ramblas market in Barcelona. To make it, special pigs are fed a diet consisting mostly of acorns. After slaughter, various parts are salted and air-dried for years, resulting in a product so delectable and tender that it fetches more than seventy dollars a pound in the United States. A dark cherry red in color, the meat is sweet yet salty with a tang of gaminess, similar to prosciutto but with more finesse and depth of flavor. We have had homemade soppresatta in Campania and Puglia, capacola in Tuscany, prosciutto in Parma, speck in Val d'Aosta, and saucisson l'ail in Chamonix. Each is distinct and wonderful. A few thin slices of salumi, a piece of rustic bread, perhaps some fruit, and a glass of wine make a damn good lunch. As a ménage à trois, these three foodstuffs are magical. There's also a practical reason for any wine bar to serve them together. As host, all I have to do is slice and pour.

It's important to point out that to be a supporter of Slow Food doesn't mean one can't appreciate food that is efficiently and quickly prepared. No one has expressed that philosophy better than food pioneer Alice Waters. In a *Platinum* magazine article by Joe Ray, she described fast-food culture as frenetic. "It's like we're in bumper cars," she told the interviewer. But that doesn't mean she wants to stand over a stove all day: "I want to cook something in a minute and eat." The difference is that her fast meal comes straight from her pantry in the form of real foods, not packaged products. And great salumi makes a quick, delicious, authentic meal.

Study It and Eat It

In chapter 8, I introduced you to Patrick Martins, founder of Heritage Foods USA. He was the one who tipped me off to Salumeria Biellese. On his advice, I placed my first salumi order with the shop. Two days later, the package arrived. I tore it open, more thrilled than a kid at Christmas. Inside were prosciutto cotto, a flavorful lean ham that had been cooked with fresh herbs and cured to perfection; fiocchetti, dried salami lovingly seasoned with fennel and other spices; traditional sweet capacola; Spanish-style Serrano ham seasoned with paprika; spicy chorizo; garlicky merguez; and sumptuous dried wild boar salami. The various dry and fresh sausages as well as the hams were all uniquely exciting. The taste differences were both distinct and subtle, and the textures were unbelievably good. These meats are almost too wonderful to put on a sandwich. I knew we had found the perfect food—and the perfect supplier—for our wine-bar menu.

So I was eager to meet the family in person, and I had a particular interest in talking to Paul Valetutti Jr., who had started a Slow Food chapter at Rutgers University, where he's a food science student. Even more intriguing, he's a pioneer in Rutgers's new degree program, culinology, a discipline that bridges the art and the science of food. The concept of culinology was introduced by the Research Chefs Association, which was founded in 1996. The group's goal is "bringing excellence to food product development," and its members include leaders in food production companies and chain restaurants. This is greatly encouraging. It shows that even leaders of large corporations are beginning to embrace the principles of unadulterated food and to recognize values that go beyond efficiency charts and cost-benefit ratios. Of course, we in the Slow Food movement believe education is key; so it's gratifying to watch Rutgers, now ranked as one of the top-five food science graduate programs in the world, keep pushing the envelope with this new discipline.

I was also looking forward to finding out more about the salumi business from Paul Valetutti Sr.—knowing, of course, that one benefit of interviewing an Italian restaurateur is that you can count on doing it over a great meal. As Kim and I walked south from Penn Station, we kept an eye out for the family's handsome restaurant, which soon came into view. Under bright-red awnings that bend around the corner of the block stands a deli-like store bustling with customers. Nearby is another entrance for the restaurant, Biricchino, where we found a large table waiting for us, set with assorted breads, olives, bruschetta, wine, and bottled water. At the head of the table was Paul Sr., wearing his signature white butcher's coat and flashing a big smile. He is always a gentleman but with street smarts found only in New York City. For many years, he has been learning and refining his products, and he is looking forward to having his children involved. Salumeria Biellese is a true love story, filled with people passionate about each other and the food that they produce. Even the family's chef, Adriano, has been with them since 1992—a great track record in an often fickle business. Such love and loyalty are vital factors in the quality and consistency of the foods they offer.

Soon platters laden with salumi began to appear at the table. And unlike the drab mass-processed salami available in most supermarkets, the colors were dazzling.

Some were deep blood-red like a rose; others were pale and white, sliced thin as silk. Some were mottled with jolly bursts of peppercorns, herbs, or nuts or were dappled and creamy with fat. That afternoon we must have sampled at least fifteen different kinds of salumi—prosciutto, prosciutto cotto, coppa, cotechino, salami, soppresatta, mortadella. Each seemed more wonderful than the last. And the wines? All were perfectly suited and in harmony with the meats.

During the meal, Kim I traded looks of awe and appreciation and the occasional nudge and whisper. Our palates were cartwheeling with pleasure, and so was our inspiration: "Yeah, this chorizo would work at the wine bar; so would the soppresatta, and how about . . . ?" In true Italian style the parade of plates kept coming, as did the wine. By now, a couple of hours had passed. Pasta arrived, one platter fixed with homemade sausage and sundried tomato, the other loaded with specialty ravioli. The meal ended with creamy tiramisu and great coffee. A perfect three-hour lunch!

So what makes Salumeria Biellese's salumi so good? Simple, the company makes its products properly: everything is handmade using all-natural ingredients and the meat from specific breeds (certain breeds have the best fat content and flavor for traditionally crafted salumi) and then naturally aged. The trade is a true craft that takes years to learn and generations to perfect. Salumeria Biellese uses Berkshire pork almost exclusively, but it's begun experimenting with several other breeds that have been raised locally. The company is already working with Simply Grazin' in Belle Meade, New Jersey, to obtain Piedmontese beef for their delicate and delicious bresaola, which is an air-dried and cured beef; and it's experimenting with the meat from several purebred hog breeds to produce huge guiancialle and flat pancetta, two types of unsmoked bacon that are classic Italian predecessors of our American-style bacon. Not only are the specific breeds important factors in the quality and consistency of the products, but the company requires everything in their salumi and sausage to be 100-percent traceable, on the infinitesimal chance that some part of the product has been contaminated.

I asked Paul how his prices compare to the large industrial salumi. "Oh, we will always be more expensive," he shrugged with a sigh. "People would not believe how stringent the standards are from the USDA. It means we must spend enormous amounts of money to be able to show that our products are safe to eat." Costs include hiring outside experts to oversee the salumi-making process. These outsiders must sign confidentiality agreements because, as part of their oversight work, they are on intimate terms with the family's secret recipes. The business also has a USDA inspector on the premises every day to ensure that it adheres to the health codes.

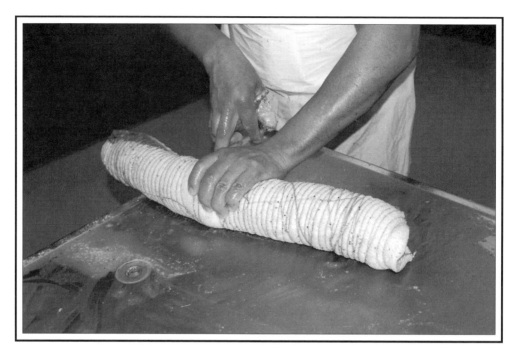

Hand rolling a pancetta
Photo by Jim Weaver

Although salami factories have these same costs, their production is much higher. While Salumeria Biellese produces approximately 15,000 pounds of product a month, the large industrial companies can produce that much *every day*. But the folks at Salumeria Biellese are willing to jump through the hoops. To prove that they are here to stay, the family recently added a new crafting and drying facility in Hackensack, New Jersey. This is where all their products are now made. They needed the new facility because demand for their provisions is growing. True salumi needs time to age properly and thus takes up space. Rents in Hackensack, I am sure, are cheaper than those in Manhattan. And now they have room to grow, which they intend to do.

When you visit the facility, the first thing you notice is its immaculately sanitized environment. Before Kim and I were allowed to enter, we had to put on starched white butcher's coats and hairnets. (Kim might love the products, but she wasn't a big fan of the fashion.) The floors are customized with special resins to reduce shoe contamination, and throughout the day special equipment automatically sprays the floors with cleaning solutions. Most of the facility is refrigerated, including the room in which the meats are processed. Large grinders and specialized stainless-steel machines line the windowless walls.

On the day of our visit we saw large Berkshire pork bellies being seasoned liberally with a blend of herbs and spices known only to a select few, although I detected bay leaf and white pepper. They are then rolled, skillfully tied by hand, and hung to age for several months. Then they are ready to eat, either just as they are or perhaps sautéed with onion, tomato, and peperoncini and tossed with freshly cooked pasta. Paul said, "We could easily speed up the process like many of the big producers do by using injectors and then cooking the meat, but it would not be the same." He leaned into one of the refrigerated racks where several hundred pancetta had been hanging for a month or so. "Can you smell that sweetness?" he asked. "Factory-made pancetta does not have that smell, and this is just one way we monitor our products."

I doubt the big factories know how to sniff out good flavor, and I am sure they have not invented a machine to do it either. Unfortunately, many American palates have become conditioned to mass-produced, salumi-like products made with the cheapest meat that can pass inspection. These supermarket varieties represent a model of efficiency, yes. But they are about as authentic as the Americanized catch-all word *salami*. To create these bastardized foods, companies employ food scientists, who test the fat content and subsidize the necessary fat with emulsifiers. The meats are then put into artificial casings and subjected to heat and tumblers. A process that should last for months is shrunk down to a few weeks. What Slow Food wants is to bring us back to the real thing.

The Salumi Mule

Today, another obstacle looms over the future of authentic salumi. The threat of airline terrorism has made it nearly impossible for chefs to bring back samples of quality salumi products from their original countries. In the past, they would routinely lug back (some might say "smuggle") samples of unique dried meats or other foods from their European homelands. The goal was to study the meats and replicate them exactly in this country. Chefs were known to sneak in everything from pork sausages in suitcases to donkey meat in the tips of their packed shoes. Though the practice has never been exactly legal, customs officials usually gave the malefactors little more than a frown and a chiding. But according to a January 2010 front-page article in the *Wall Street Journal*, this informal practice has been virtually abolished. Today, contraband salumi is treated as if it's a bomb component. When Kim and I returned from a trip to Spain, every single suitcase on our plane

Meats aging at Salumeria Biellese in Hackensack

Photo by Jim Weaver

was hand-searched in a special room at Newark Liberty International Airport. Thankfully we did not have any contraband food.

Some chefs are fighting back by seeking an educational exemption that would allow them to bring in small samples of unique meats for study and replication. But thanks to Salumeria Biellese, which has had an eighty-year head start, many of the traditional recipes from Biella and the Piedmont region don't need to be smuggled in. They are already here. It's gratifying to realize that, years before the Slow Food movement was founded, this family was already introducing the American palate to traditional food that reflected the philosophies of Slow Food. The family anticipated many of the things that the movement has come to stand for: the business is sustainable, its products are traceable, its methods are traditional, and it's filling a niche market. In short, Salumeria Biellese and its restaurant, Biricchino, have refined the art of serving happy food to happy customers. No wonder that Paul Valetutti and his staff are among the most convivial people I have ever met. And what do our customer at the Tre Bar think? "More salumi, please."

ᔷ

Following are a couple of recipes. The first has nothing to do with salumi. It does, however, relate to sneaking in foods from overseas. I first ate this tuna at a restaurant where I worked, just outside of Milan, and the chef gave me a half-gallon jar to pack in my suitcase and take home to America. The tuna had been aged for more than six months, and it was delicious. Canned tuna in oil pales in comparison. It's a great example of how time can be a crucial ingredient in many recipes, including, of course, salumi.

The second recipe calls for Salumeria Biellese cotechino. Cotechino is a traditional northern Italian garlic sausage that is semi-cured. It is part of the region's traditional New Year's Day meal and should be served with baby lentils. Lore has it that if you partake in this feast, good luck will be bestowed upon you.

Tonno sott Olio (Tuna under Oil)

Makes 2 quarts

2 pounds fresh tuna loin
3 cups white wine
3 cloves garlic
I cup white-wine vinegar
3 tbsp. kosher salt
I tbsp. black peppercorns
2 lemons
4 cups extra-virgin olive oil
4 bay leaves

Wrap tuna loin in cheesecloth and secure with kitchen twine.

In a large pot, combine the wine, garlic, vinegar, salt, pepper, lemons, and juice. Add I cup of the olive oil. Bring to a simmer and add the tuna. Cook about 10 minutes per inch of thickness or until the center reaches 130 degrees. Remove from heat, and let the tuna cool overnight in the cooking liquid.

The next day clean two quart-sized canning jars, and boil them to sterilize. Remove the tuna from its liquid, unwrap the cheesecloth, and trim off any skin, bones, and bloodlines. Cut the tuna into the largest-sized pieces that will fit into a jar. Pack into each jar fairly tightly. Cover the packed tuna with the rest of the oil, and place a bay leaf on top.

Place the jars in a large deep pot and fill with water almost to the top of the jars. Bring the water to a simmer and cook until the internal temperature reaches 130 degrees. Clean the tops of the jars with a dry towel and place the canning lids on. Secure with the bands and remove from the water. Let cool and check that the lids have sealed. Refrigerate until ready to use, up to a year.

- - - - - - - -

Salumeria Biellese Cotechino over Green Lentils

Serves 4

1 cotechino (approximately 2 pounds)
¼ pound pancetta, cut into large chunks
2 carrots, 1 peeled and left whole, 1 peeled and finely chopped
2 medium-sized onions, 1 peeled and halved, 1 peeled and finely chopped
2 celery stalks, 1 whole, 1 finely chopped
4 garlic cloves, 1 peeled and left whole 1 peeled and minced
1 pound green lentils, picked over and rinsed
2 cups chicken broth (you may need slightly more or less)
2 tsp. aged balsamic vinegar
1 tbsp. unsalted butter
Sea salt
Freshly ground black pepper

In a large pot, cover the cotechino in water, and let it stand in the refrigerator for 1 to 2 hours. Once the sausage has come to room temperature, place the pot on the stove, and bring it up to a slow simmer. (High heat will cause the casing to rupture.) Cook the sausage slowly for 1½ hours.

In a medium-sized saucepan with a lid, render the fat from the pancetta over medium heat. Cook the pancetta in the fat until it becomes crispy. Then add the whole carrot, the halved onion, the whole celery stalk, and the whole garlic clove, and cook them until they begin to color. Stir in the lentils. Now add enough chicken broth so that the lentils are barely covered. Loosely cover the pot, and cook for about 45 minutes or until the lentils are al dente. Remove from the heat, and stir in the vinegar and the butter. When the butter has melted, season with salt and pepper. (*Note:* Be careful not to oversalt the lentils. Cotechino is semi-cured, which means that it is much saltier than fresh sausage.) Remove the whole vegetables, and let the lentils sit off heat to absorb the remaining liquid.

In a small pan, briefly sauté the finely chopped vegetables over low heat, and add them to the lentils.

Once the cotechino has finished cooking, slice it into ¼-inch thick rounds. To serve, spoon some lentils onto each plate, and arrange slices of cotechino on top.

Biricchini Restaurant and Salumeria Biellese
376–378 Eighth Avenue
New York, NY 10001
(212) 736–7376
http://www.salumeriabiellese.com

10

Foie Gras Adventure

Foie gras has been treasured for centuries—enjoyed by ancient pharaohs and enshrined in French law. Its mellifluous name rolls off the tongue like warm butter off a china plate. Some say it may be the first gourmet food invented by humans. Yet its back story is not for the faint of heart. Foie gras translates as "fat liver," and for most fans of foie gras, the technicalities of how this delicate remnant of duck ends up on the plate is better left to the pros. What makes it memorable is its taste and texture. Here are a few descriptive samples from the many Internet bloggers who have struggled to capture its elusive character. "Like the crispy fat on the edge of a grilled steak," writes one. "Rich and buttery," says another. Yet though its charms are hard to pin down, everything else about foie gras is clear—or is it?

Time to Chew the Fat

The truth is that foie gras is the result of force feeding ducks or geese for several weeks to plump up their livers. At the close of this gastronomic orgy, the bird is slaughtered and the foie gras is harvested. This procedure, called *gavage*, has produced a classic and noble foodstuff for at least 4,000 years. Chef Anthony Bourdain calls it "one of the ten most important flavors in gastronomy." Yet animal-rights advocates have condemned gavage as cruel, and numerous nations have now banned foie gras production, including Germany, the United Kingdom, and Switzerland. In several U.S. cities and states, there has been ongoing pressure to ban foie gras from restaurant menus—among them San Diego and Chicago and the entire state of California. Although Slow Food USA has not taken an official stance on foie gras, the International Slow Food website does protect and promote French foie gras because it is important part of that nation's history and culture.

Recently, as I headed north from Princeton toward the rolling hills of Sulli-van County, New York, I found myself thinking about the complexities of foie gras. At last count, there are only four production houses in the United States, and I was heading for one of them: Hudson Valley Foie Gras, the nation's largest producer, processing 4,000 to 6,000 ducks a week. It is my local source for foie gras as well as the source for most fine-dining restaurants on the east coast. At Tre Piani, we are proud to serve Hudson Valley's product. No matter that we specialize in Italian cuisine—foie gras is a classic foodstuff and is a jewel in the crown of any fine-dining experience.

The ancient Egyptians are credited with first discovering foie gras. They had observed that ducks gorged themselves to fatten up for long migratory flights. And when those birds were killed for food, the pharaoh's chefs noticed that the fatty livers looked particularly succulent. But France is the country that has adopted foie gras as its own cultural icon. There was a day when any four-star French restaurant would have been called unworthy of the name without foie gras on the menu. Yet it has always been tricky to prepare. Much as I support and encourage the tradition of home cooking, the preparation of foie gras is extremely technical; and unless you know what you're doing, you will end up with a greasy mess (although, for the undaunted, I've added some good recipes at the end of this chapter).

Because I love foie gras yet also understand the controversies surrounding it, I'm eager to see Hudson Valley Foie Gras in action. This award-winning farm is a pacesetter in the use of humane and high-tech production methods. What's more, its owners are true lovers of the delicacy and are committed to producing a high-quality product made from animals that have been treated in a civilized and enlightened way. The company is nestled in the hills of Sullivan County, about twelve miles from the site of the legendary 1969 Woodstock rock festival. Today, you'll find bed-and-breakfasts, hunting and fishing camps, lakeside views, farms, and antique shops. And you'll also find two guys who've set out to create a humane and responsible business that would supply customers with a great culinary classic.

The landscape profile of Hudson Valley Foie Gras is so unobtrusive that, when you arrive, you might think you've driven up to the barn of a very well tended mom-and-pop farm. Clean, white, low-slung buildings are spread across wide lawns dotted with paths and groves of large shade trees. Inside the barns, sunlight streams through the windows, and the ducks waddle about freely, looking as content as the 4-H livestock exhibits at your local state fair.

Yet the owners of Hudson Valley Foie Gras, Izzy Yanay and Michael Aeyal Ginor, have backgrounds as unusual as their product. Izzy came to the United States from Israel in the early 1980s, bringing with him the Moulard duck, an

Moulard ducks
Photo by Jim Weaver

innovative hybrid that is particularly well suited for foie gras. Despite a résumé that includes a stint as manager for Israel's largest foie gras producer, Izzy is a bit of a renaissance man. Not only is he recognized as a worldwide authority in foie gras operations, but he's also earned degrees in film, philosophy, and agriculture. Yet foie gras has always been a passion.

His future business partner, Michael Aeyal Ginor, began his career on Wall Street. A Seattle native, he is the son of Israeli immigrants, a heritage that eventually inspired Michael to leave the corporate world to join the Israel Defense Forces. But inside, a true foodie lurked, waiting to break out. Since his return to the United States, Michael has gathered a long list of culinary awards and has developed workshops, festivals, and demonstrations to thrill the heart of every gastronome. He's also an author, and his latest book is *Foie Gras: A Passion*.

At the center of Hudson Valley's success is the Moulard duck, a crossbreed that produces an excellent and uniform quality of foie gras. This hybrid, a cross between a Muscovy male and a Pekin female, was invented in Taiwan hundreds of years ago, but the breed was refined and brought to Israel in the 1970s because it was hardier and more disease-resistant than either of its parents. When Izzy began farming with the Moulard in 1981, he was, for quite a while, the only producer of foie gras in the United States. Yet his business remained small until 1991, when he met Michael and they joined forces to form Hudson Valley Foie Gras.

Today, two decades later, the company distributes nationally through gourmet and specialty food distributors. Its products have won a string of awards from around the world, including prizes from the James Beard Foundation and the American Tasting Institute. Its website lays out the company mission: "Our corporate goals include the stabilizing of Foie Gras prices and the assurance of a steady supply as well as public education and increased product awareness. In keeping with our promise to develop a more economic high-quality product, a significant portion of our proceeds is directed toward research and development."

The Fly in the Foie Gras

For Izzy and Michael, the foie gras operation is a labor of love. Yet when love is involved, can heartbreak be far behind? Enter the armies of animal-rights activists, who have waged a battle to stop the production of foie gras everywhere in the world. Even though Hudson Valley has been dedicated since the beginning to using humane methods in the production of this classic, the company has still come under attack. The point of contention is gavage—the process of force feeding the ducks to produce a fatty liver.

So what's the truth? Is foie gras production a legitimate, humane business, or is it duck torture? For an answer, you could hardly ask a more skeptical investigator than a reporter for the *Village Voice*. Yet in a February 2009 article headlined "Is Foie Gras Torture?" Sarah DiGregorio wrote that her visit to Hudson Valley's operation proved to her that foie gras operations could be done in an enlightened and humane way. Before she arrived, DiGregorio had been armed with an arsenal of arguments and background material from animal-rights organizations. Among the materials were videos (not taken at Hudson Valley) of what were called "tortured ducks." And, as the reporter pointed out, if torture were truly part of foie gras operations, no sane person should support it, wherever it might happen. But she went on to write: "Those images are not representative of the reality at the nation's largest foie gras farm. . . . If I had seen with my own eyes that Hudson Valley produced foie gras by abusing ducks, this article would have turned out very differently. But that just wasn't the case."

I was anxious to see the operation with my own eyes, and fortunately Izzy Yanay is a gregarious tour guide. As he describes the farm's operations and how his ducks are treated, his hands flap around wildly. Izzy says that he spends most of his time giving farm tours, which are free of charge for any group of five or fewer, but only if they make advance arrangements. When I contacted him, he enthusiastically agreed to let me interview him and take photos. He even agreed to sign a release so I could write about what I saw. In the half-day I spent with Izzy, he showed me every inch of the farm, including the entire process of raising the ducks: from their hatching, to their move to larger pens, to their constant watering and feeding. I even saw the controversial parts of the operation: gavage, slaughter, processing, and packaging. What I learned is that Hudson Valley's operation is more or less similar to any other small- or medium-sized free-range poultry farm's. The only difference is the gavage, a three-week process that takes place just before slaughter. Although Izzy is the first to admit that gavage is not a natural process, I saw absolutely no evidence that any bird suffered, or even objected, to being force fed.

The livers that result from gavage are five to six times larger than the liver of a duck that has not gone through the process. Here's how it works: in a ten-second procedure, a worker inserts a long feeding tube down the length of a duck's neck, which allows the bird to quickly ingest an enormous amount of food. The insertion procedure is repeated several times a day for about three weeks, when the duck reaches the proper size for slaughter. Gavage may sound like torture until you learn something about the physiology of ducks and geese. Unlike humans, they don't have a gag reflex. What's more, the tubing doesn't hurt: their throats are made of such a tough substance that they can even swallow a whole fish—bones, fins, teeth, and all. Finally, ducks breathe through their tongues, which means that they can swallow food and breathe at the same time.

"Yes, it is true we force-feed ducks by putting a 'cold, hard, steel tube' down their throats," Izzy says, emphasizing the animal-rights activists' inflammatory verbiage. "We feed them a diet heavy with carbohydrates in the form of corn. It is also true we do not use local corn as the local corn is no good for our purposes. So it is all true—we are not hiding anything." The mockery in Izzy's tone shows that he's heard all of these arguments before. And now that I've seen the operation for myself, I can testify that the animals I watched were not being treated cruelly.

We have to remember that virtually all the animals we eat must be raised in specific ways to produce food. It's also important to understand that ducks are different from mammals. Like many birds, they naturally gorge themselves before they migrate or hunker down for a hard winter. So even in the wild, without human intervention, ducks gorge themselves to store up energy, which takes the form of fat in the liver. The difference is that ducks raised for food are killed before they get a chance to use their stored energy. Okay, gavage is probably not as fun as paddling in a pond; but on the other hand, these pampered ducks never have to worry about being hungry or thirsty or left to fend for themselves in the harsh elements. Their health and comfort matters to Izzy. As he explains, "if they die, I lose money. My ducks are raised cage-free, are well fed, and have access to fresh water at all times."

Nonetheless, opposition to foie gras is growing, and only a handful of countries still permit its production, including, at last count, France, Belgium, Spain, and Hungary, as well as the United States and China. Even though foie gras production is legal in this country, Hudson Valley Foie Gras has faced a barrage of lawsuits filed periodically by a large animal-protection organization. Though Izzy says the farm has successfully fended them off, the costs have been high.

Of course, to some people, killing any animal for food is cruel. But most human beings recognize that's an unrealistic goal and hasn't been the norm since humans first emerged from the caves, spears in hand. Don't forget that animals even get killed every day at certified organic vegetable farms. On these farms, many birds, insects, and other animals are considered pests and have to be eliminated so that the farmers can deliver wholesome produce to the table. Why, anyone who has driven a car or walked down a sidewalk has cooperated in the deaths of thousands of insects!

I wish the activists would consider that their stated goal—to save animals—is actually *enhanced* by humane food production. The best example is the work of Heritage Foods USA, which, as I've shown in previous chapters, has one of the most enlightened and humane animal-preservation missions in the world. Its slogan "to save them, we must eat them" is a reminder that, in the natural order of things, many wildlife and livestock breeds thrive precisely because they are treasured as foodstuffs. Another major animal-rights goal is to liberate animals from their human "oppressors." But as I showed in chapter 5, when activists broke into Griggstown Quail Farm and sent George Rude's free-range birds into the "freedom" of the wild, all of the "liberated" animals promptly died. As many animal science experts have noted, the lives of animals in the wild are far more stressful than those of humanely treated farm animals. Hudson Valley's manager, Marcus Henley, told Sarah DiGregorio of the *Village Voice* that animal activists want people to believe that Hudson Valley is running a "horror chamber." But the charge doesn't stand up: "We have national-level vets come visit; we have journalists and chefs. How am I going to trick these people?"

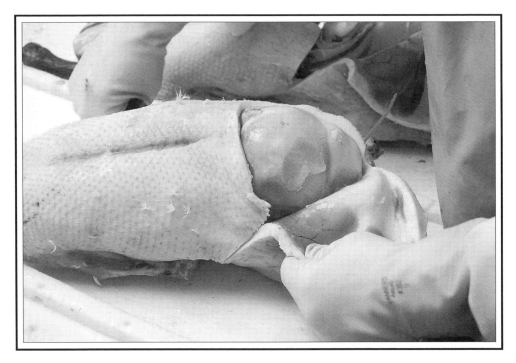

Processing foie gras
Photo by Jim Weaver

For her article, DiGregorio asked several livestock experts to share their thoughts about foie gras production. Among them she interviewed Temple Grandin, a prominent animal sciences professor and the pioneer inventor of a humane cattle chute. Grandin confirmed the hardy physiology of the duck species and said, although she had never visited a foie gras farm, she didn't consider them to be inherently wrong. I agree. And I also agree that treating these birds well results in superb foie gras. Among the many fans of Hudson Valley's product is Chef Anthony Bourdain. On a visit to the farm, which he recorded for YouTube, he made a spirited defense of this noble foodstuff, praising it as "one of the most delicious foods on earth." He's right!

∽

Following are several recipes for duck and foie gras, which Michael Ginor, chef at Hudson Valley Foie Gras, shared with me.

Grenadine-Cured Magret Duck Breast, with Celeriac Mousseline, Pomegranate Glaze, Chervil Salad, and Seared Hudson Valley Foie Gras

Serves 4

GRENADINE-CURED MAGRET DUCK BREAST:

½ cup grenadine syrup

2 cups water

2 ounces coarse sea salt

2 ounces brown sugar

2 bay leaves

5 peppercorns

2 cloves garlic, peeled

2 Magret duck breasts, split, rinsed, patted dry with the skin on, and scored diagonally

1–2 tbsp. canola oil

CELERIAC MOUSSELINE:

I large celeriac, peeled and roughly cubed

2 cups heavy cream

Coarse sea salt

Freshly ground white pepper

POMEGRANATE GLAZE:

3 pomegranates (or I cup unsweetened presqueezed juice, available in specialty markets)

3 tbsp. sugar

CHERVIL SALAD:

I cup chervil

½ cup pomegranate seeds

Fresh lemon juice

Coarse sea salt

Freshly ground black pepper

Sea salt for garnish

SEARED HUDSON VALLEY FOIE GRAS:

I lobe (about I pound) fresh, grade-A Hudson Valley foie gras, cut into 4 steaks

Coarse sea salt

Freshly ground black pepper

FOR THE DUCK BREAST: In a large stockpot, combine all the ingredients except the duck breasts and the vegetable oil. Bring to a boil. Remove from heat, and cool completely. Cover the duck breasts with the cooled brine, and marinate in the refrigerator for 3 to 5 days, depending on the desired degree of curing.

Remove breasts from the liquid. Rinse and pat dry. Keep at room temperature while preparing rest of dish.

FOR THE CELERIAC MOUSSELINE: In a heavy pot, cook the celeriac cubes in the cream until tender. Drain the cubes, reserving the cream. In a blender, blend the celeriac with about ½ cup of the cream until smooth. The texture should lie between a puree and a creamy sauce. Pass through a sieve. Season with salt and pepper. Reserve and keep warm. Use the same day.

FOR THE POMEGRANATE GLAZE: To make your own pomegranate juice, carefully remove the seeds, puree them in a blender, and then strain out the liquid.

In a small saucepan, combine the pomegranate juice and sugar. Over low heat, simmer about 20 minutes or until the liquid has reduced to a glaze. Remove from heat and set aside.

FOR THE CHERVIL SALAD: Toss the chervil with the pomegranate seeds, a splash of fresh lemon juice, salt, and pepper. Set aside.

TO FINISH THE DUCK BREASTS AND PREPARE THE FOIE GRAS: Twenty minutes before serving, heat two pans on low-medium heat. Add I tbsp. vegetable oil. Heat the duck breasts skin side down to render the fat slowly, about 10 minutes. Turn over and cook an additional 3 to 5 minutes. Remove from heat, cover completely, and let rest for 5 minutes. Slice to serve.

Score one side of each foie gras steak in a cross-hatch pattern with a sharp paring knife. Season both sides liberally with salt and pepper. Heat a dry skillet on medium-high heat. When very hot, add foie gras slices and sear about 45 seconds. Turn over and cook another 45 seconds, until medium rare. Remove slices, drain on paper towels. Prepare to serve immediately.

TO ASSEMBLE: Ladle celeriac mousseline onto the middle of heated plates. Top with slices of duck breast. Place a foie gras steak on top of the duck. Top the foie gras with chervil salad, making sure each plate has a fair portion of pomegranate seeds. Drizzle pomegranate glaze around the plate. Sprinkle a few grains of sea salt over the dish. Serve immediately.

Pan-Seared Squab Breasts and Foie Gras, with Beet Glaze, Port Demiglace, Parsnip Mousseline, and Herbed Salad Garnish

Serves 4

BEET GLAZE:
4 beets, juiced (you'll need a juicer
    to extract the juice)
2 tsp. sea salt
I tsp. freshly ground black pepper

PORT DEMIGLACE:
½ cup squab or veal demiglace, or rich
    stock reduced to a syrupy consistency
I bottle port wine, reduced by four-fifths
Sea salt
Freshly ground black pepper

PARSNIP MOUSSELINE:
2 pounds parsnips, peeled and cut
    into small pieces
½ cup heavy cream
Kosher salt
Freshly ground white pepper

HERBED SALAD GARNISH:
3 ounces chervil or microgreens,
    carefully washed and dried
Half a lemon
Kosher salt
Freshly ground black pepper

PAN-SEARED SQUAB BREASTS AND FOIE GRAS:
4 medallions of Hudson Valley foie gras, about 3 ounces each
4 squab breasts (this equals the breasts of two squabs)
Kosher salt
Freshly ground black pepper
I tsp. canola oil

FOR THE BEET GLAZE: Combine the beet juice, salt, and pepper in a stockpot and reduce over medium heat to a glaze. Set aside.

FOR THE PORT DEMIGLACE: Over medium heat, combine the demiglace (or reduced stock) and the reduced port wine. Season with salt and pepper. Set aside but keep warm.

FOR THE PARSNIP MOUSSELINE: In a heavy-bottomed pan, combine the parsnips with enough cream to cover them. Bring to a simmer over medium heat. Then reduce the heat to low and cook until the parsnips are soft, about 90 minutes. Strain, reserving the liquid. Place the parsnips in a blender. Add ¼ cup of the reserved cooking cream, and blend until very smooth. The consistency should be thinner than a puree but light and fluffy. Add more cream if necessary, and season to taste. Set aside, keeping the mousseline warm in a water bath.

FOR THE HERBED SALAD GARNISH: In a bowl, gently toss the chervil or microgreens with a squirt of lemon juice and a touch of salt and pepper. Set aside.

FOR THE PAN-SEARED SQUAB BREASTS AND FOIE GRAS: In a warm oven, preheat 4 large dinner plates.

Score one side of each foie gras medallion in a crosshatch pattern with a sharp paring knife. Season both sides liberally with salt and pepper. Set aside.

Season the squab breast with salt and pepper. Heat the oil in a sauté pan over medium-high heat. Add the breasts, and cook for about 2 minutes per side.

Meanwhile, heat a dry skillet over medium-high heat. Add the foie gras medallions and sear for about 30 seconds. Turn over and cook for another 30 seconds. The medallions will be medium rare. Remove the foie gras and drain on paper towels. Serve immediately.

TO ASSEMBLE: Remove the dinner plates from the warm oven. For each serving, brush a stroke of beet glaze across the plate. Place a mound of parsnip mousseline in the center. Pull a slice of seared foie gras through the reserved warm port demiglace, and lay the medallion on top of the mousseline. Now pull a seared squab breast through the port demiglace, and lay it on top of the foie gras. Finally, top the breast with a pinch of the herbed salad garnish.

Michael Ginor's Duck Cholent

Serves 8–10

This cholent, also known as Jewish cassoulet, contains various parts of the duck. You may choose to use any or all, or you can substitute various beef cuts.

2 Magret duck breasts with skin intact, about 2 pounds
1 tbsp. coarse sea salt
1 tbsp. freshly ground black pepper
1 tbsp. duck fat or chicken fat

2 tbsp. duck fat or chicken fat
4 pieces Zvia Ginor's derma (recipe follows)
4 duck or chicken sausages (storebought)

8 ounces smoked duck breast (storebought), finely chopped
3 large yellow onions, chopped into medium dice
2 tomatoes, quartered
½ cup brown sugar

8 cured duck legs (recipe follows)
16 cured duck gizzards (recipe follows)
1 cup dried cranberry beans
1 cup dried great northern or other white beans
2 cups finely diced celery root
5 sprigs fresh thyme
2 bay leaves
1 head garlic, trimmed but intact
8 raw eggs, in the shell
3 quarts cold water or chicken stock

Preheat the oven to 225 degrees.

Season the duck breasts on both sides with salt and pepper. Over medium heat, melt 1 tbsp. duck or chicken fat. When the fat is hot, brown the duck breasts, skin side down, for about 10 minutes. Turn over the breasts and cook on other side for about 3 minutes. Remove meat from pan, and it cut into large cubes. Set aside.

In a Dutch oven or a cholent pot, melt 2 tbsps. duck or chicken fat. When the fat is hot, add the derma and sausages, and sauté on both sides until golden brown: about 5 minutes for the sausage and 10 minutes for derma. Remove the meat. Leave derma whole, but slice the sausages on a diagonal so that they are about ¼ of an inch thick.

Return the Dutch oven or cholent pot to medium heat. Add the smoked duck breast. Sauté for I minute. Add chopped onions and sauté until translucent, 5 to 7 minutes. After 4 minutes add the tomatoes and brown sugar. Stir and finish cooking for about 10 minutes.

On top of the onion mixture, place duck breast cubes, the derma, the sausage slices, the cured duck legs, and the cured duck gizzards. Top the meat with beans, celery root, thyme, bay leaves, and the garlic head. Arrange whole eggs in the shell around the top of the pot.

Add enough cold water or chicken stock to the pot to cover the contents. Bring to a boil, cover the pot, and place it in the oven. Cook for a minimum of 4 hours and maximum of 8. Make sure there is enough liquid in the pot at all times. You can make cholent in the evening and let it cook overnight.

Remove from oven. Let cool slightly. Remove the eggs as soon as they are cool enough to handle. Peel them, and return them whole to the pot. Serve the cholent immediately, or cool it completely to store. To reheat, cook slowly on top of stove over very low heat, stirring occasionally. Or heat in the oven at 250 degrees.

When you serve, be sure that each guest has some of every element in the pot.

· · ·

Zvia Ginor's Derma

Serves 8

4 duck neck skins	2 celery ribs, finely diced
¼ cup duck fat or chicken fat	¾ cup all-purpose flour
Coarse sea salt	2 tbsp. bread crumbs
Freshly ground black pepper	I tsp. chopped parsley
I medium onion, minced	Boiling salted water

Wash and clean the neck skins inside and out. Season inside and out with salt and pepper. Tie the narrow end of each with butcher's string.

In a small skillet, melt the duck or chicken fat over low heat, and sauté the onion and celery until they are soft and the onion is lightly browned.

In a mixing bowl, sift the flour with a pinch of salt and pepper. Add the bread crumbs. Stir in the sautéed onion and celery mixture, and add the parsley. Mix well and loosely stuff each neck skin. (Be careful not to overstuff.) Tie up the open ends.

Immerse the derma in boiling water for 3 to 5 minutes. Drain. Set aside to be browned later.

Duck Leg and Gizzard Confit

Serves 8

8 duck legs
16 fresh duck gizzards, trimmed
I cup coarse sea salt
2 tbsp. freshly ground black pepper
½ cup brown sugar

2 tsp. chopped fresh thyme
2 tsp. chopped fresh rosemary
2 bay leaves, crushed
¼ cup brandy
I large garlic head, lightly pounded
 but whole

Place the duck legs and gizzards in a large shallow dish. Combine salt, pepper, brown sugar, thyme, rosemary, bay leaves, and brandy. Rub the spice mixture thoroughly into the meat. Bury the garlic in the meat. Refrigerate, covered, for 24 hours.

Remove from refrigerator. Brush or rinse off the spice rub. Pat dry with paper towels. Proceed with cholent recipe.

ↄ RESOURCES

Hudson Valley sells all the duck products listed in this chapter's recipes:

Hudson Valley Foie Gras
 (877) 289–3643

Products are also available at many specialty shops and markets, including:

D'Artagnan
 http://www.dartagnan.com

Michael Ginor has two restaurants:

Lola
 II3A Middle Neck Road
 Great Neck, NY II023
 (516) 466–5666

Anise
 6I3 Middle Neck Road
 Great Neck, NY II023
 (516) 466–6136

11

Educating the Classes

A school cafeteria doesn't sound like the kind of place where Slow Food reigns. Most young people eat fast food, right? They crave fats and carbs and will scarf through any pizza, no matter how processed. Vegetables? About as popular as a pair of out-of-style jeans. So you know something new is going on when a cafeteria full of high school students gives you a standing ovation for introducing them to Slow Food, including fresh vegetables.

That's what happened to Gary Giberson, executive director of dining at the Lawrenceville School in Lawrenceville, New Jersey. The private school, whose roots go back two hundred years, is known for innovative social programs such as its green campus initiative. Slow Food might seem to be a natural fit here. But it's one thing to learn about the concept of supporting a food economy that is local, sustainable, and environmentally sound. It's another to put that food on a teenager's plate. That's what Gary did, and the students' standing ovation was how they thanked him.

Gary began working at the school in 1998, when the food service company that provided Lawrenceville's meals hired him as executive chef. But as he discovered, food service companies deal mostly with processed food. "Even though the Lawrenceville School was open to innovation, I felt like I was in a straitjacket," Gary says. So he decided to start his own food service business, one with a very different goal: to bring only fresh, seasonal fare to hospital cafeterias, company lunchrooms, and dining halls filled with skeptical teenagers. Although Gary didn't launch his own business until 2007, he'd already starting introducing a sustainable fare menu to those Lawrenceville teens. And far from pelting him with tomatoes, the kids were eating them up. It turned out they loved the new menu. So much for the myth of veggies as a natural kid repellent. "No, kids *do* like vegetables," Gary says. "It's just that no one has given them the opportunity to have them in the correct way!"

Education, Coast to Coast

Gary says he's a chef by trade and a business owner by necessity. Like the rest of us, once he got the Slow Food concept, he couldn't go back. He describes his company, Sustainable Fare LLC, as an environmentally responsible food service; and in a few short years he has built a roster of clients across the country, including both public and private schools. Among his many other pursuits, Gary teaches independent-study courses on cooking and using local, fresh, sustainable food products. His urge to educate is a vital contribution to Slow Food because our ability to inspire the next generation is what will set the future course of the movement.

Today, more and more food businesses, including farms and restaurants, are making Slow Food education a key part of their public outreach. For example, school garden projects are springing up all over the place. In Brooklyn, New York, an old baseball park has become a working garden where kids are paid to farm. Innovations such as farm camps take kids into rural areas to learn directly from the pros. In the mid-1990s, Alice Waters established the Edible Schoolyard (ESY), a program of the Chez Panisse Foundation. It's a one-acre organic garden and kitchen classroom for an urban public school near her restaurant. These middle school students may be growing up in an atmosphere of cement-bounded parks and fast-food joints, but once inside the Edible Schoolyard, they enter another world. There, they become actual participants in the growing, harvesting, and preparing of fresh, seasonal produce. Imagine how inspirational it would be for urban kids to watch their own efforts make real food happen.

Now another famous restaurant is putting its educational stamp on the surroundings. Co-owned by Dan Barber and his brother David Barber, Blue Hill is one of the great eating places in New York City. The Barbers are pioneers in the farm-to-table approach to restaurant cooking; and Dan has earned many awards and recognitions, including the honor, in 2009, of being named the country's best chef by the James Beard Foundation. His new educational venture is Blue Hill at Stone Barns, which has opened within the Stone Barns Center for Food and Agriculture in Pocantico Hills, New York, just thirty miles north of New York City. Here the Barbers have created a working, four-season farm that is open to the public. Its mission is "to create a consciousness about the effect of everyday food choices." Under the trademark "Know Thy Farmer!" the Barbers are educating people about the abundant food choices of the Hudson Valley. Visitors to Stone Barns can browse in a farmers' market, attend appearances by food authors, and chat with local farmers. What's more, they can dine "with" the Barbers, which is an eye- and palate-opener, whether you're in New York City or the rural Hudson Valley.

In Hunterdon County, New Jersey, a farm named Bobolink Dairy has become one of the latest go-to places for people to learn about and enjoy fresh, sustainable products. The farm is run by farmers and master cheesemakers Nina White and Jonathan White. It offers internships and apprenticeships in cheese- and breadmaking, grass-based milk production, and more. The education component of Bobolink Farm has not only advanced the Slow Food philosophy but has also helped to preserve the farm's very existence.

Not long ago, this historic, two-hundred-acre farm, which had changed hands only twice since the American Revolution, was in danger of being sold off for development after the death of its longtime owner. Instead, the farm became part of the Hunterdon County Land Trust, which will preserve it as an educational and working farm forever. With the Whites in charge, that means the public has ongoing access to a lively and varied curriculum. And because they also have an autistic son, Jacob, they are deeply involved in promoting and educating the public about the relationship of food to disabilities such as autism. As part of their educational mission, the Whites are helping persons with disabilities to become farmers and food producers.

The Perfect Sustainable Storm

Gary Giberson was already an experienced chef before he began cooking at the Lawrenceville School. After an apprenticeship at the legendary Warwick Hotel in Philadelphia, he served as chef de cuisine at the prestigious Rams Head Inn in Absecon, New Jersey. That expertise served him well in the food service industry. But as he became more involved in the Slow Food movement, even the practices at an enlightened institution such as Lawrenceville made him increasingly dissatisfied. "At the time no one was talking sustainability. It was more about providing a service," he says. The idea of locally grown food wasn't on the company's radar screen. Rather, its business model focused on efficiency and the negotiation of favorable prices.

Gary, however, had begun to hang around with guys like Dr. Kevin Lyons, director of purchasing at Rutgers University, an expert in environmentally sound purchasing practices. One of Dr. Lyons's most intriguing areas of research was discovering where foods came from. He began literally at ground zero: a landfill. From there, he documented where the discarded food trash had gotten its start.

Autumn gourds at the market

Photo by Pegi Ballister-Howells

Fishing boats at rest at Viking Village

Photo by Jim Weaver

Heirloom tomatoes at the farmers' market

Photo by Jim Weaver

Man versus monkfish at Viking Village

Photo by Jim Weaver

Radishes at the farmers' market

Photo by Jim Weaver

Wall of Fame at the Bent Spoon

Photo by Jim Weaver

Broad-Breasted White turkeys

Photo by Jim Weaver

Sign for Cherry Grove Farm

Photo by Jim Weaver

Berkshire pig

Photograph by Jen Munkvold

Stone Barns Berkshire pig with late summer vegetables

Photo by Antoinette Bruno

Bourbon Red turkeys

Photo by Jim Weaver

Union Square farmers' market

Photo by Jim Weaver

Sign for Valley Shepherd Creamery

Photo by Jim Weaver

End of the season at the Lawrenceville Elementary School garden

Photo by Jim Weaver

Soon he was sharing his fascinating, out-of-the-box thinking with students at Lawrenceville.

Gary was also getting to know the leaders of the Slow Food movement, including well-known sustainable-living advocate Judy Wicks, creator of the Sustainable Business Network and the Fair Food Project as well as many other groups. He met Erika Lesser, executive director of Slow Food USA and a longtime leader in the organization. Their inspiration fused with his own deep beliefs, and suddenly he knew that change was possible: "I believe the moment I realized that what I was doing could have an impact on the health of students, and also on the planet, that was a key moment. Then, to be talking to all the right people, and all of us talking the same language—well, that was like the perfect sustainable storm. It was a real light-bulb moment for me."

Not long afterward, Gary and his wife, Lisa, found themselves in Rome. It was New Year's Eve 2005, and that night the couple celebrated in a restaurant over plates of prosciutto and melon. "The melons were never sweeter; the prosciutto was perfect," Gary remembers. It was an unforgettable night capped with unforgettable food. The next day he came back to the restaurant, planning to re-create the experience. But when he ordered melon, the waiter told him they were gone. At first, Gary thought his Italian was at fault, so he tried again, in his best Italian accent. No, shrugged the waiter, the melons were no longer available. The night before had been the end of the season for melons.

"I realized I had eaten the last melon in Rome," Gary says. "That was an epiphany for me." In America, no one ever stops to think about the melons one is eating; after all, they are usually available, if not always memorable. But in Italy, the tradition is to eat the food when, and only when, it's seasonally fresh. The idea is entrancing and powerful. For Gary, that New Year's moment concentrated everything he already knew about Slow Food into one big-picture moment.

Food Feedback

But do those moments stick? Do they really lead to lifestyle changes? Maybe they do if you're an accomplished chef spending a memorable night in Rome, but what if you're a kid trapped in a school cafeteria? After all, kids have to eat what's put in front of them, especially if their parents are paying the freight. Can good cafeteria food change lives?

Gary chuckles: "Every year I get e-mails from college students who are sorry they ever thought of complaining about the food." That's because, once they leave any of Gary's client schools, they discover the sorry state of cafeteria food in the real world. Most college cafeterias are uneducated outposts of processed food, but the students from Gary's schools are still craving the fresh foods he prepared for them. As he puts it, these are kids who "get *excited* when we serve asparagus."

How exactly do Gary and other Slow Food advocates manage to bring fresh food to huge crowds of people on a daily basis? "First, I analyze where the food is coming from," Gary says. "It all starts with buying as locally and sustainably as possible." That means not just produce but also pasta, meat, and seafood. In addition, Gary analyzes each kitchen's capabilities. Many times, kitchens are built specifically to accommodate high-fat processed food. So to create a food service that honors Slow Food, the kitchen must be turned into a place for cooking, not a place for heating up large quantities of frozen food.

Gary challenges his clients—including the students—to read food labels. This way they can discover for themselves that a frozen burrito has more than fifty ingredients, including some that are close to unpronounceable. How many ingredients are in a fresh burrito? "You have beans and cheese and some fresh vegetables in a tortilla. You don't need any more than that."

Gary Giberson
with sustainably raised
salmon portions
for hundreds of hungry
Lawrenceville School
students

Photo by Jim Weaver

But school trustees and other school authorities need to control costs, and they are constantly worried about the expense of serving fresh, local, seasonal foods. Gary has an answer: look at the difference in waste. Kids throw away more processed food simply because it doesn't taste as good. Moreover, costs are contained when you buy food in season, which is when it's cheapest. When you have to ship in, say, tomatoes from Mexico or Florida, you're spending more money.

Regarding cost control, Gary has a few other tricks up his sleeve. "We take a holistic approach," he says. For example, in a standard food service operation, the approach is to tote up how many people—say, 1,000—will be eating at that meal service. Cooking starts at 10 A.M., and the food is kept in a warmer until the crowds come and get it. But Gary uses batch cooking techniques. That is, instead of cooking for everyone at once, he cooks for fifty people, and then fifty more people, and so on. By keeping records of a crowd's predictable ebb and flow, he can make sure that every person has access to a fresh, delicious meal.

Imagine, for instance, that a kitchen staff has fifty pounds of Swiss chard available for a lunchtime crowd. Under the old method, workers might cook the whole fifty pounds of chard at one time. As the crowd ebbs, the uneaten chard slowly shrivels in the food warmer. By the time the next surge of people arrives, it's just another dreary example of old-style cafeteria food. According to Gary's method, staff members wash and cut up only as much chard as they need for a single batch of customers. Then they cook the cleaned chard with garlic and olive oil just before the first lunchtime surge arrives so that it's hot, fresh, and inviting. They repeat the process for each predicted surge of eaters. The chard that doesn't get cooked will be used the next day for a soup or a salad. These uncooked portions remain edible and tasty, unlike the reheated glop that in some cafeterias masquerades as a next-day meal.

Perhaps Gary's most dramatic move has been the elimination of cafeteria trays, a change that has reduced food waste by an amazing 22 percent. How? If kids have trays, they fill them up and then leave a large portion of that food untouched and destined for the garbage pail. In Gary's method, the students can carry only a plate and a drink back to their table: "If they want more, they have to come back." It took some doing, he says, to persuade school authorities to ditch the trays. But after a one-week trial period, they realized he was right. The trays were history.

Cooking for Carlo

In 2008, Gary was asked to host Slow Food founder Carlo Petrini's visit to the Lawrenceville School. By this time, Gary was a Slow Food veteran. He had already served as a chef delegate to the organization's annual Terra Madre conference in Torino, and his work at Lawrenceville was well known. Carlo was traveling in America to promote a new book about Slow Food, and he wanted to eat lunch with the students. The founder spent five hours on campus, touring and eating. His favorite food that day? The gazpacho. Through his interpreter, he joked to Gary that the food at the Lawrenceville cafeteria was much better than what he'd eaten the night before in a New York restaurant.

If only everything about Slow Food was as easy as cooking for Carlo! But Gary continues to find that old traditions are hard to break. For example, his Sustainable Fare food service business may win a school client as part of a grant program; but if the grant isn't renewed, his program can't continue at the school. Invariably, he must work his way through a maze of demands and needs, most of which spring from school boards and unions that support opposing agendas. "It's a very slippery slope getting involved with school budgets," Gary says.

But there's power in banding together. These days Gary is working with Ann Cooper, a chef and high-profile Slow Food advocate also known as the Renegade Lunch Lady. Ann's mission is to improve the food that kids eat in school. "No more talking—start doing!" as she writes on her lively blog. And she's right: the one constant seems to be "feed the kids right, and they will come." As Gary explains, "We want to educate kids about all the practices—from fair housing to fair food—that will allow them to become the leaders of tomorrow, and give them the understanding necessary to be successful in the workplace. No matter what job you get, if you understand the concept of sustainability, you will have a better chance of succeeding. And a lot of kids care."

ॐ

Following are a couple of recipes that show up on Gary Giberson's Sustainable Fare food service menu.

Couscous and Tomato Salad

Serves 4 to 6

8 ounces couscous
8 ounces hot vegetable stock
1 medium-sized red pepper, seeded and diced into ¼-inch pieces
1 medium-sized tomato, seeded and diced into ¼-inch pieces
1 cup broccoli florets, blanched and finely chopped
½ cup minced red onion
Sea salt
Freshly ground black pepper
¼ cup olive oil
Juice of 1 lemon

In a large bowl, stir together the couscous and the hot vegetable stock. Let the mixture sit for 10 minutes, or until all the liquid has been absorbed.

Add the remaining ingredients and toss. The salad may be served immediately or stored in the refrigerator for up to 3 days.

Butternut Squash and Apple Bisque

Serves 4

1 butternut squash, peeled, seeded, and diced into 1-inch cubes
(about 2 cups)
3 medium-sized apples, peeled, seeded, and diced into 1-inch cubes
(about 1½ cups)
1 onion, coarsely diced (about ⅓ cup)
1 carrot, peeled, coarsely diced (about ⅓ cup)
1½ cups vegetable stock
1 dash cayenne pepper
2 dashes ground cinnamon
1 dash ground nutmeg
⅓ cup heavy cream
4 tbsp. sour cream
1 tbsp. sliced chives
Sea salt

Combine the squash, apples, onions, carrots, and stock in a heavy sauce pan, and bring to a boil over high heat. Reduce the heat to medium, and simmer for about 20 minutes, or until the squash is very tender. Remove the pot from the heat and let cool. Then puree the mixture in a blender. (You may prepare the recipe in advance up to this point. Refrigerate in a covered container for up to 3 days.)

Return the puree to the saucepan and turn the heat to medium-low. Stir in the heavy cream, cayenne, cinnamon, and nutmeg. Taste and adjust seasoning if needed. Heat to a simmer; do not let soup boil. Keep warm until ready to serve.

Ladle soup into warm bowls and garnish with sour cream and chives.

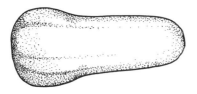

Sustainable Fare
(609) 620–6143
http://www.sustainablefare.com

Bobolink Dairy
(908) 86GRASS
http://www.cowsoutside.com

Ann Cooper's blog
http://www.chefann.com

Edible Schoolyard
http://www.edibleschoolyard.org

Stone Barns Center for Food and Agriculture
630 Bedford Road
Pocantico Hills, NY 10591
(914) 366–6200
http://www.stonebarnscenter.org

12

Viking Village

If you want to understand the New Jersey seafood industry, Viking Village is a good place to go to look at the big picture. Since the 1920s, this historic outpost, located at the northern point of Long Beach Island, has been at the center of New Jersey's commercial fishing industry. A major producer, Viking Village sits in the town of Barnegat Light, a tiny spit of ocean-hugged real estate. From here, it sends more than 5 million pounds of seafood all over the world every year—a very significant contribution to the state economy. It also continues to evolve its mission as a supporter of modern, environmentally sound fishing practices that work in tandem with a good business model. "We've worked really hard with sustainability issues across the board and in cooperative research," says general manager Ernie Panacek. He's the son-in-law of the legendary John Larson, known throughout the New Jersey fishing industry as "Cap'n John," the deep-sea fisherman who headed Viking Village for many years before he passed away in late 2009.

A supporter of the Slow Food movement, Viking Village has sponsored dock tours, luncheons, and held educational Slow Food events. The company's manifesto, written by Ernie, is prominently displayed on its website: "At Viking Village, we take pride in being leaders in a program emphasizing responsibly caught fish and scallops, ensuring minimal impact on the environment and fish habitat. We continue to work closely with the National Marine Fisheries Service and play a major role in the management and cooperative research process."

Barnegat Light, home of Viking Village, is surrounded by the waters of the Atlantic and Barnegat Bay, and the town is accessible only by way of the causeway bridge on Route 72. With a winter population of slightly more than seven hundred residents, this is about as far from urban New Jersey as you can get. Yet thanks to its deep harbor, Barnegat Light has become one of the state's six major fishing ports. Clearly, the seaworthy Scandinavian immigrants who settled this place had found an address that felt like home.

You may be surprised to learn that, among states on the eastern seaboard, New Jersey is second only to Massachusetts in the amount of seafood it harvests annually. Sure, people may be more familiar with the high-profile branding of Maine lobster and Maryland crab. But New Jersey harvests millions of pounds of fresh, top-quality fish and shellfish every year. As I discussed in chapter 3, the Cape May Salt oyster has a premier culinary reputation, but many of us also believe that New Jersey sea scallops can hold their own on any menu. As a matter of fact, even though New Jersey has been justifiably labeled "the Garden State," it could just as easily have been called "the Fishing State." Since 1692, when Barnegat Light was mentioned in a 1692 deed from the English Crown, the region has been engaged in a commercial seafood harvest. And centuries before the Europeans arrived, local tribes depended on the bountiful fresh fish and shellfish in our ocean, rivers, marshes, and tributaries.

Today, there's a huge, unofficial, but cooperative effort among all interested parties to make sure that the New Jersey fishing industry survives. From restaurant owners, to foodies, to university professors, to trawler captains, supporters of the industry are working to preserve our unique seafood heritage. The stakes are high. For one thing, there's the sheer importance of preserving a vital foodstuff. And then there's the economic impact of the state's commercial and recreational fisheries and aquaculture. With an annual value of $4.5 billion, the industry affects the well-being of every New Jersey man, woman, and child.

As I've discussed throughout this book, Rutgers University is a key player in keeping the state's food industries viable. In addition to all the work it does with land-based agriculture, the university has instituted a number of innovative programs to support the state's irreplaceable fisheries, from mollusks to mahi mahi and everything in between. Its New Jersey Agricultural Experiment Station (NJAES) has become a clearinghouse for the state's entire seafood industry, whether one is looking for information, research material, or outreach activities. You can find answers there to nearly any question, from "How many fish live in the sea off the New Jersey coast?" to "What are the latest environmental concerns about scallop dredging?" With Rutgers's cooperation, the industry has constant access to best practices for staying both commercially viable and environmentally sound. For instance, to address the lack of training facilities for commercial fisherman who want to learn the latest seafood aquatic techniques, Rutgers created the Multispecies Aquaculture Demonstration Facility, which dedicates more than 22,000 square feet of space and 120,000 gallons of seawater solely to the raising and study of finfish and shellfish.

Viking Village tilefish boat

Photo by Jim Weaver

Seafood Meets Slow Food, New Jersey Style

If you want to see the Slow Food philosophy in action, visit a New Jersey fishing port. Nothing's hidden behind six blocks of factory walls or processed three states away from the harvest. What you see is what you get. First, the fishermen come into port and offload their catch. Then the fresh seafood is iced down, graded, and weighed. Within hours it's hauled away to various markets. These same steps are repeated every day.

New Jersey's harbors are home to more than 1,500 commercial fishing vessels, so there's a lot of seafood to handle. Much of each day's haul is sold fresh, but some also gets shipped for processing to one of the state's fifteen or so plants specializing in frozen fish filets, cleaned squid, or clam juice and strips. New Jersey is the world's largest producer of sea clams: the kind that are often sold as cheap, fried clam strips but that are also used for canned chopped clams and clam juice. (As a chef and Slow Food advocate, I can't resist throwing in my two cents here: while these processed clams may be adding millions of dollars to our state economy, I don't think they're so good for our culinary image.)

The areas surrounding these working harbors hum with related businesses, such as shipbuilding, boat repair shops, and other support services. They're also beginning to hum with eco-tourists. These are visitors whose travels are inspired by an interest in the natural world, including foods grown and harvested at their source, and the Slow Food movement is eager to educate them. At our New Jersey harbors, these visitors can see firsthand the methods and the energy behind the harvest of many of their favorite foods: oysters, clams, lobsters, crabs, tilefish, swordfish, monkfish, tuna, fluke, flounder, mahi mahi, squid, sea scallops, scup . . . the list goes on and on.

Industry leaders such as Viking Village's Ernie Panacek understand the importance of catering to eco-tourists and other discerning visitors: "Today you need a better, higher-quality product. You need more boats making shorter trips and bringing their catch home faster. This cuts the time between catch and consumption, giving consumers a better-tasting, safer, and higher-quality product than ever before." Certainly, the ante has been upped in the competition for high-quality fish. I heard recently that, in Japan, a single giant bluefin tuna sold for more than 150,000 dollars. So it's not simply a question of "Will there be enough fish in the sea?" but "Will there be enough of the most sought-after fish in the sea?"

To keep up with demand, the seafood industry has plunged wholeheartedly into the business of farm-raised fish. In this process, saltwater fish are nurtured in giant netted areas set up in the open sea, whereas freshwater varieties are raised on land in giant tanks. Some observers see farming as a good alternative to extinction by overfishing. But detractors are concerned that farmed fish have an overly high fat content and carry concentrated toxins such as PCBs, which may cause cancer. They argue that unsanitary farming conditions spread parasites and disease and that farm-raised fish exude excessive nutrients, which create dead zones in ocean water.

Among the most popular farmed species are salmon, cod, carp, striped bass, and trout. If you order tilapia, branzino, or catfish, you're also likely to get a farmed variety. Many people believe that the "farm-raised" label indicates they're buying a product that's consistently sized, less expensive, and sustainably grown. But as a chef, I find that the taste of farmed fish pales in comparison to the flavor of their wild cousins. I believe my Tre Piani customers can taste the difference as well.

Government Regulations : Not under Threat of Extinction

I'm proud that New Jersey is a national leader in quality seafood and that it has evolved in its environmental knowledge, appreciation of local processing, and standards of food production. This is the Slow Food movement philosophy at its seafaring best. Recently another movement has actively engaged not only Viking Village but also the entire U.S. fishing industry, whose members have joined together to fight what they see as rigid government regulations that are cramping the business of seafood management.

In February 2010, fishermen from across the country converged on Washington, D.C., in an attempt to untangle this net. At the heart of their complaint was the Magnuson-Stevens Fishery Conservation Act of 1996, meant to ensure that species are protected from overfishing, unsound harvesting practices, and possible extinction—all elements that the fishing industry supports. But despite acknowledging the good intentions behind the act, the industry believes that fishing stocks are now so overmanaged that the nation's commercial and recreational fisheries have been severely crippled. "They're regulating us out of business," Ernie Panacek says. "We all want the fish stocks to prosper and be around for future generations." He agrees that, yes, years ago, "the stocks were overfished. But today I think we're overemphasizing that the stock's in trouble. We've been fighting off these excessive regulatory controls, and it takes up a lot of our time."

A major sore point is the provision that requires fishermen to allow virtually all species to reach a certain restock level within a ten-year span of protection. But according to the industry, this requirement has resulted in numerous unintended consequences, all of them bad. One is that certain destructive species now swim under regulatory protection, which has allowed them to multiply and overtake eatable species. For example, New Jersey fisheries are now struggling to deal with a voracious predator known as the spiny dogfish. The industry argues that no species was designed to live out its life cycle under an artificial ten-year armistice. This is a total disruption of the food chain. As Ernie puts it, "they *eat* each other! *Hello!* We're unbalancing the eco-system."

"The key," he says, "is to base the regulations on science, not politics." In other words, the laws need to reflect the flexibility of nature. "We want to make Congress aware that they need to act on this soon. Commercial fisheries and the recreational fishing industry are suffering desperately." I agree with Ernie. Though regulation of seafood is necessary, it should not be based on poor science or, as sometimes happens, be applied arbitrarily, depending on which adversary has the better lobbyist. Rules change from state to state, and the United States controls the seas only up to two hundred miles offshore. After that, it's open season on almost anything that lives below the waves.

The day's catch at Viking Village, ready to ship

Photo by Jim Weaver

Here's a regulatory example from my own life. When I was a kid I spent most of my summers on Cape Cod. My father and grandfather were avid fishermen, and we spent many a day on the bay fishing for striped bass. I remember the three of us bringing in dozens of huge stripers and bluefish. Both species are exciting to catch and great to eat, although the bass was the clear favorite in my family. My father usually ended up with coolers full of bluefish fillets that he would give away to his friends. They were about as well received as a holiday fruit cake.

As the years passed, we noted that we weren't catching as many striped bass in the bay and that the ones that we did manage to haul in were of inferior size compared to the fifty-plus-pound giants we used to catch regularly. Not long afterward, some states began regulating the recreational industry, and obviously it was necessary. But even today, years later, stripers are still regulated in New Jersey. Commercial fisherman, seafood markets, and restaurants are not allowed anywhere near them, although in New York and Pennsylvania you can catch and eat stripers anywhere. Oh, I can get the farm-raised variety, but that would be like substituting Velveeta for Vermont cheddar. The stripes aren't even straight on the farmed stripers, and the flesh has neither the texture nor depth of flavor of the wild fish.

But is this regulation still necessary? It's a difficult question. How do you regulate migratory animals that live below the waves when you can't really see how many are down there? Does a mish-mash, state-by-state method of regulation really help a species, or does it just make it more difficult for a fisherman to earn a living? Who should make these decisions, and how do we enforce the rules? What's best for the fish themselves? There seem to be no perfect answers.

Scallops: A Success Story

But there are also success stories in the regulatory world, and sea scallops are one of them. Scallops are a huge part of the New Jersey seafood experience, and they account for half or more of Viking Village's haul. Fortunately, they are solely a commercial commodity: scallops aren't hunted for recreation.

Sea scallops are caught by dredging. Fishermen drag what is basically a giant rake along the sea floor. The rake is ingeniously designed to catch mature sea scallops and let the younger, smaller ones slip by. New regulations recently required that rakes have tines spread even farther apart, and many scallop fishermen instantly opposed the idea. But within a few years, they realized that the sea scallops they were harvesting were larger and more plentiful than they had been before the new rake regulations were set. As a result, fisheries were actually able to lower prices and significantly raise the quality of the product.

Many environmentalists abhor the practice of dragging a giant rake along the sea bottom for miles at a time, and it's not hard to see why. Think of the destruction such a rake could do as it passed over sea corals and naturally growing seabeds. But as Nils Stolpe explains, sometimes worries are misplaced: from the mid-Atlantic states to Florida, the ocean floor is basically sand, meaning that it has no reefs, coral beds, or any other oceanic architecture that could be damaged by a rake.

Stolpe is a major figure in the world of New Jersey fishing. The magazine *National Fisherman* has dubbed him "New Jersey's Giant" and "the U.S. Fishing Industry's One-Man Think-Tank." Stolpe is a hero in the industry because of his clear and cogent defense of commercial fishing. A New Jersey native, he developed his interest in all things aquatic as he earned degrees at Rutgers University in environmental science and environmental planning. According to *National Fisherman,* the state hired him to develop a master plan in aquaculture for New Jersey, but he resigned from the job because he bristled at the bureaucracy and the high costs of implementation. Today, as an independent consultant for fisheries, he's found the freedom to work for the industry from the inside out.

Scallop-dredging rig at Viking Village
Photo by Jim Weaver

"Nils is such a good writer in laying out ideas and [in] the factual basis he relies on," says Jim Lovgren, a fourth-generation commercial fisherman from Point Pleasant Beach, who was quoted in the *National Fisherman* article. According to Lovgren, who is a leader at the Garden State Seafood Association, where Stolpe does communications work, "we've had Nils working for the [New Jersey fishing] industry, but everything he does is also benefiting the industry around the country."

I was interested in Stolpe's conclusions about scallop dredging. After all, scallops have a place of honor on Tre Piani's menu: they are tucked into our spicy angel hair pasta and our panzanella salad, and they star in one of our main dishes—sea scallops sautéed in a pignolia nut crust. Scallops are a staple of our New Jersey food harvest and a load-bearing wall of our economy. I wanted to see scallop dredging myself and draw my own conclusions about it. So why not ask one of my commercial fishing friends if I could join him on a trip to harvest sea scallops?

"Sorry, buddy, can't do it," my friend Danny Cohen from Cape May said. "No guests on the boats. Regulations." It turns out that, by law, scallop boats can carry only a limited number of people. The reason is that fewer people on a boat means fewer scallops harvested. In addition, scallop season is limited to a certain number of days and to a certain number of hours within those days. Think you might nudge the rules to stay out a little longer? No way. Each boat carries a satellite tracking device, a "black box" that's monitored by regulators. Once the vessel passes the invisible boundary that defines the scallop beds, the device starts timing the fishermen. If they stay out too long, they are heavily fined. They'd also better be careful not to go over the number of pounds caught. In short, a modern sea scallop operation is no place to be shooting the breeze with a buddy who's just along for the ride.

ᘒ

Here are a few of my favorite ways to serve New Jersey seafood. I've also included a recipe from Will Mooney, chef and co-owner of the Brothers Moon in Hopewell, New Jersey.

Garden State Seafood Panzanella Salad

Serves 2

1 large baguette
½ cup diced Jersey tomato
½ cucumber, julienne-cut or (preferably) cut on a mandoline to resemble spaghetti
¼ fennel bulb, trimmed, cored, and julienne-cut (reserve a few fronds for garnish)
1 scallion cut on the bias into thin slices (reserve the green top for garnish)
3 ounces monkfish
8 littleneck clams
4 large sea scallops
1 squid (about 3 ounces after cleaning)
½ cup extra-virgin olive oil
2 garlic cloves, peeled and sliced
½ tsp. sea salt
Freshly ground black pepper
6 basil leaves, 4 sliced into chiffonade, 2 reserved whole for garnish
1 cup water
3 tsp. lemon juice

PREPARING THE BAGUETTE: Remove the crust, and cut the soft interior into ½-inch cubes. Lightly toast the cubes in a preheated 350-degree oven. Set aside. (You will need about ½ cup of toasted bread cubes for the recipe. If desired, the rest of the bread can be used for an optional garnish; see below.)

FOR THE VEGETABLES: In a large bowl, combine all the prepared vegetables except for the garnishes. Keep chilled until ready to use.

FOR THE SEAFOOD: Skin the monkfish, and cut it into bite-sized pieces. Rinse the clams of any sand. Peel the abductor muscle from the sides of the sea scallops. Peel and clean the squid. Pull the tentacles and everything attached to them out of the tube. Cut the tentacles off just above from where they start, and discard the beak and eyes. Also remove the tough, clear membrane from within the tube and discard. Slice the squid into ¼-inch rings. Keep the seafood chilled until it's all ready to cook.

Heat a large sauté pan over a medium flame and add the olive oil. Season the scallops and monkfish with salt and pepper, and sear until browned on the outside. Remove from the oil, and set aside. Add the garlic to the pan, and let it brown slightly. Add the squid rings, and give them a quick toss. Next add the clams and the water. Season lightly with salt and pepper. Cover the pan until the clams begin to open, and then return the scallops and monkfish to the mixture. Cook, covered, until all the clams open, or about 1 minute. You may have to add more water if the clams do not open. You just want to make sure that you have about ½ cup of liquid left when the cooking is finished.

TO ASSEMBLE: Remove the cut vegetables from the refrigerator. Add the basil, and season with salt and pepper. Now add the toasted bread cubes and toss. Just before serving, toss in the hot seafood and half of the cooking liquid.

Divide the seafood mixture onto plates. Garnish with the scallion sprigs, fennel fronds, and basil leaves, and pour the remaining seafood broth around each plate. Serve immediately.

OPTIONAL BREAD GARNISH: You'll need to make these ahead of time. Slice the leftover baguette lengthwise into 2 ¼-inch-thick slices. Grease 2 metal ring molds with olive oil, and wrap a bread slice around each. Tie them with kitchen string, set the molds on a small baking sheet, and bake in a preheated 350-degree oven until golden. Remove the sheet from the oven, and set the molds aside until cool.

Cut the string, and carefully remove the bread from the molds. When you're ready to serve, set a mold in the center of each plate and fill it with some of the salad for a dramatic presentation.

Pignolia Nut—Crusted Sea Scallops
with Honey Lemon Beurre Blanc

Serves 2 as an entrée, 4 as an appetizer

PIGNOLIA NUT—CRUSTED SEA SCALLOPS:
½ cup pignolia nuts, finely chopped
¼ cup unseasoned breadcrumbs
10 large sea scallops
½ cup all-purpose flour
Sea salt
Freshly ground black pepper
3 beaten eggs
¼ cup extra-virgin olive oil

HONEY LEMON BEURRE BLANC:
1 cup white wine
2 tbsp. honey
Juice of 1 lemon
1 tsp. chopped fresh parsley
4 tbsp. butter, cut into small
    pieces and chilled

FOR THE PIGNOLIA NUT—CRUSTED SEA SCALLOPS: Combine the pignolia nuts and breadcrumbs, and reserve in a work bowl. Season the scallops with salt and pepper and lightly coat with flour. Dip each scallop in the egg; then coat with the nut mixture.

FOR THE HONEY LEMON BEURRE BLANC: Combine the wine, lemon, and honey in a saucepan and reduce over high heat until only ⅛ cup of liquid is left. Remove from heat and whisk in the parsley and butter. Set aside in a warm (not hot) place until ready to serve.

TO FINISH THE DISH: Preheat the oven to 350 degrees. On the stovetop, heat the olive oil in a large skillet over a medium flame, and add the scallops. Brown on all sides and remove to a cookie sheet. Bake the scallops in the preheated oven until done, approximately 10 minutes.

Spoon some of the sauce onto each serving plate, and top it with the hot scallops.

. . .

New Jersey Blackfish Meunière with
Poached Cape May Salt Oysters, Tomato-Cucumber Concasse,
Cilantro Broth, Garlic Croutons, and Spicy Oil

Serves 4

SPICY OIL:
¼ cup extra-virgin olive oil
2 tsp. crushed red chilies

TOMATO-CUCUMBER CONCASSE:
2 medium tomatoes
1 cucumber or ½ hothouse cucumber
Sea salt

BLACKFISH AND STOCK:
1 whole blackfish (also called tautog),
    about 4 pounds
1 yellow onion
2 stalks celery
2 bay leaves
2 sprigs fresh thyme
2 cloves
1 cup white wine

GARLIC CROUTONS:
8 slices Italian panella
2 cloves garlic
¼ cup extra-virgin olive oil

MEUNIÈRE PREP AND POACHED CAPE MAY SALT OYSTERS:
4 tbsp. butter
Sea salt
Freshly ground black pepper
½ cup all-purpose flour
16 Cape May Salt oysters, shucked, liquor reserved
2 tbsp. chopped fresh cilantro (plus a few whole leaves for garnish)

FOR THE SPICY OIL: Place ¼ cup of the olive oil and the crushed chilies in a blender. Blend at high speed, and set aside.

FOR THE BLACKFISH AND STOCK: Filet the blackfish, skin it, remove the small bones, and cut it into 6-ounce pieces. Set aside in the refrigerate until ready to cook.

Chop the bones. Put them into a large pot, cover them with cold water, and bring to a simmer. Skim the top of the stock when film accumulates on the surface. After the stock has become somewhat clear, add the onion, celery, bay leaves, thyme, cloves, and white wine. Simmer for another 30 minutes. Strain and reserve the stock.

FOR THE TOMATO-CUCUMBER CONCASSE: Bring a medium-sized pot of water to a boil, and blanch the tomatoes in it for about 30 seconds, or until the skin cracks.

Remove and immediately chill the tomatoes in ice water. Drain. Then peel and seed the tomatoes and chop them into medium-sized dice. Next, peel and seed the cucumber and chop it into medium-sized dice. In a bowl, combine the tomato and cucumber. Season with salt to taste, and set aside at room temperature.

FOR THE GARLIC CROUTONS: Cut 16 small round croutons (1 to 2 inches across) from the panella, and sauté in ¼ cup of olive oil until brown on one side. Crush the garlic and add it to the pan. Turn over the croutons, and let them brown on the other side. Remove the croutons to a platter, and drizzle them with the leftover garlic oil in the pan. Set aside.

FOR THE BLACKFISH MEUNIÈRE AND THE POACHED CAPE MAY SALT OYSTERS: Melt the butter over medium heat in a large sauté pan. Meanwhile, season the reserved fish fillets on both sides with salt and pepper. Dredge them in flour, shaking off any excess. When the butter is lightly browned, add the fillets to the pan. Cook until well browned and crisp on either side, or until just barely cooked through. Remove them to warm serving plates, and keep them warm.

Pour 12 ounces of the reserved fish stock into a second pan. Over high heat, reduce it by half. Add the oysters, their liquor, and the chopped cilantro. Poach for 30 seconds.

TO ASSEMBLE: Surround each fillet with four croutons. Place an oyster on top of each crouton. Spoon some of the reduced broth over all. Top the fish with the concasse. Garnish with a drizzle of spicy oil and a piece of fresh cilantro leaf. Serve immediately.

Seared Tuna with Sesame Vegetable Slaw

Will Mooney, the Brothers Moon Restaurant

Serves 8

SESAME VEGETABLE SLAW:
I carrot, peeled and julienne-cut
2 stalks celery, cut thinly on the bias
½ cup snow peas, julienne-cut
I red pepper, julienne-cut
¼ head Napa cabbage or romaine
      lettuce, julienne-cut
2 scallions, cut thinly on the bias
3 tbsp. mixed black and white
      sesame seeds
Sea salt
Freshly ground black pepper

SEARED TUNA:
2–8 6-ounce tuna steaks
6 tbsp. cracked black pepper
2 tbsp. sea salt
2 tbsp. canola oil

SESAME MARINADE:
½ cup rice wine vinegar
¼ cup soy sauce
I tsp. honey
I tbsp. chopped fresh cilantro
3 oz. mae ploy (sweet chili sauce,
      available at the Brothers
      Moon Restaurant)
I tsp. grated fresh ginger
I tsp. crushed fresh garlic clove
¼ tsp. sesame oil
¾ cup canola oil

FOR THE SESAME VEGETABLE SLAW: In a large bowl, combine all ingredients. Set aside.

FOR THE SESAME MARINADE: In a blender, combine all ingredients except for the sesame and canola oils in blender. While the blender is running, drizzle in the oils. Set aside. (This marinade is also good on noodles, and it keeps well in the refrigerator for several weeks.)

FOR THE SEARED TUNA: Preheat oven to 350 degrees.

Coat tuna pieces with salt and pepper. On the stovetop, heat the canola oil in a thick-bottomed sauté pan over medium heat. Add the tuna, and sear it on all sides. Remove it to a baking pan, and bake to desired doneness. *Important note:* If you like your tuna very rare, no oven time is required. The steaks will cook through quickly in the oven, so check them every couple minutes until they have reached your preferred level of doneness.

TO ASSEMBLE: Pour I cup of marinade into the slaw. Toss to coat vegetables thoroughly. Divide the vegetable slaw among the serving plates, and top with the tuna.

⅋ RESOURCES

Viking Village
    http://www.vikingvillage.net

You can find links to numerous Rutgers University research and informational centers here:

New Jersey Agricultural Experimental Station
    http://www.njaes.rutgers.edu

You can read Nils Stolpe's writings here:

Garden State Seafood Association
    http://www.fishingnj.org

FishNet USA
    http://www.fish-netusa.com

Go here for a list of species at risk of extinction:

Greenpeace
    http://www.greenpeace.org

Go here for a list of species that are safe to eat:

Monterey Bay Aquarium
    http://www.montereybayaquarium.org

13

The Best-Possible Canvas

Celebrated chef Dan Barber says that "to be a great chef is to be able to control." He means control over what goes on *in* the kitchen as well as what comes *into* the kitchen—namely, the food. You may remember that I introduced you to Dan in chapter 11. He's the executive chef and co-owner of Blue Hill, a top-tier restaurant in New York City. And since 2004, he's also co-owned and operated Blue Hill at Stone Barns, located inside the Stone Barns Center for Food and Agriculture, which is an innovative nonprofit farm and education center about twenty miles north of the city in Westchester County, New York.

As a fellow chef who is also immersed in the Slow Food movement, I wanted to see how Dan meets the issues that I, too, face every day at my own restaurant. So I headed out on a sweet spring day to join him at Blue Hill at Stone Barns, set amid the Stone Barns Center's eighty acres of working farmland, fields, pastures, and buildings set in the rolling hills of the Hudson Valley. The surroundings couldn't be more different from Dan's original enterprise, Blue Hill, which is located on the lower floor of a townhouse, a former speakeasy in the New York City's West Village. But in both town and country, Dan brings the Slow Food philosophy to the table.

Thinking Like a Farmer

In Westchester County, Dan, along with his brother David and other members of the Barber family, owns the eighty-seat restaurant Blue Hill at Stone Barns and operates the casual Blue Hill Café. The restaurant is housed in a place that at one time was a working dairy barn on the Rockefeller estate. When David Rockefeller and his daughter, Peggy Dulany, decided to establish the Stone Barns Center as an educational center offering classes focused on farm-to-table eating, gardening workshops, and programs for children and families, they also decided they wanted a restaurant—but not an everyday one. Blue Hill seemed like a great fit. In New

Chef Dan Barber
on the farm
at Stone Barns

Photo by
Andrew Hetherington

York City, Blue Hill has long been known for its casual elegance, lack of preten-
sion, and comparatively affordability. Today, in both venues, the restaurant's menu
remains dedicated to featuring the freshest seasonal food available.

The Stone Barns idea began as an experiment. When the center opened in
2004, *New York Times* reporter Neil Genzlinger decided to write a piece about it for
Food & Wine magazine. At the time, he summed it up as "a $30 million experiment
in reconnecting people to what they eat." But since then, the enterprise, founded
on land that Rockefeller's grandfather, industrialist John D. Rockefeller, acquired
a hundred years ago, has grown more than anyone might have anticipated, thanks
to strong philanthropic support and a lot of public interest.

Because I, like Dan, own a restaurant, I'm familiar with the issues we both face
in running a food and hospitality business. But I'm definitely not a farmer, and

neither is he. Yet as a member of the Stone Barns Center's board of directors and chair of its program committee, Dan is learning to *think* like a farmer. He's also got farming in his blood. His restaurant is named after his grandmother's Blue Hill Farm in Great Barrington, Massachusetts, where he spent many happy childhood days. In a 2007 interview for the Institute of Culinary Education, Dan talked about his experiences on the family farm: "Blue Hill Farm is strikingly beautiful, and in part that's because of my grandmother's desire to keep the open space, to keep that a farm. With that beauty comes kind a responsibility. I think she gave me that sense of responsibility because I was put to work. And so that must have translated into my feelings about food, which is to some extent the responsibility attached to the way we eat, or in the place that we eat, or for myself, in the way that we cook."

Dan Barber is one of the most down-to-earth professionals I know. But he's also a great chef. Kim and I have dined several times at both restaurants, and every visit was stupendous. Blue Hill at Stone Barns does not have a menu, and we've always been happy to leave the entire meal in the chef's hands. Our first dining experience there began with fresh pea burgers. This whimsical dish starts with a thick puree of peas, picked only hours before. They are presented on miniature olive oil *financiers* (small, bun-like cakes), which are baked in-house. Fresh snipped baby vegetables and herbs came next—no accompaniment needed. This deceptively simple dish says more about Slow Food than any twenty-page treatise could: food tastes best when its properly grown and harvested. Later in that same meal we had freshly baked toasted red fife brioche with freshly made ricotta ladled on top. Also on the menu: veal marrow bones with paddlefish roe, lamb's tongue, pork shoulder, and onions that had been cooked for hours near an outdoor wood-burning grill and served with dipping sauces. Four courses of cheeses and desserts rounded out the sublime meal. The final tab was more than 600 dollars.

Learning from the Masters

Like others involved with the Slow Food movement, chefs and restaurant owners work to encourage a sustainable food economy that allows people to enjoy food in its natural state—locally harvested, seasonal, and grown without artificial, mass-production techniques. Dan Barber has gone a step further: at Blue Hill at Stone Barns, he's drawn aside the curtain to show how he acquires his ingredients and develops his dishes. For example, instead of presenting diners with a traditional menu, he offers them a sampling of up to one hundred seasonal ingredients. What

Dining room at Blue Hill at Stone Barns

Photograph by Jonathan Young

he prepares changes daily, depending on what's in season and being harvested that day. This straightforward philosophy about food has brought him both success and professional honors. He's earned a number of best-chef awards, including one from the James Beard Foundation; and in 2009, *Time* magazine named him as one of the hundred most influential people in the world. In the fullest way, Dan is putting into practice the ideas that Carlo Petrini first set out when he launched Slow Food International more than twenty years ago: that ecology, geology, nutrition, and environmentalism are intertwined and that you cannot really be an expert in any of those disciplines unless you are a gastronomist as well.

But the cook's connection to the farmer is a crucial link. As Carlo said in a more recent interview, "today hardly anyone buys their wine directly from their trusted wine maker, or goes to the farm to buy eggs and a chicken or a rabbit; hardly anybody knows the baker who makes their bread, the charcutier who slaughters the pigs and cures the meat, the man who churns the milk of his sheep or goats to make cheese." This must change, and the farmers agree. Wendell Berry, a Kentucky-born author, poet, and farmer, has been touting sustainable agriculture and local husbandry for decades. As he says, "eating is an agricultural act."

Yet it's also important not to idealize farming. Many of my farmer friends object to the hazy, romantic glow that floats around the public image of sustainable family farming. In an effort to promote country life, writers sometimes manage to make the business of farming sound like an effortless romp through the Garden of Eden. The farmers themselves know better. They are realistic, tough-minded people who deal with the real world from the trenches. Especially in areas with high land values, they constantly struggle with the complex formula of success. How do they set a price that will guarantee a return on their investment? How do they address the high costs of transportation, state regulations, ongoing educational commitments? And how do they also find time to harvest and raise quality foods?

Seeing Is Believing

Maybe you've heard the expression "a great meal begins with the eyes." That's how I felt as I drove closer and closer to Blue Hill at Stone Barns. Its setting of rolling hills and pasture is truly majestic, "a model for a Winslow Homer painting," as Neil Genzlinger wrote in his *Food & Wine* article. The place had a great deal of personal meaning for David Rockefeller, which is why he wanted to turn eighty acres of his family estate into a working farm. His late wife, Peggy, had been a passionate advocate of local farming, and he felt that Stone Barns was a good way to honor her memory.

Rockefeller's original plan was to open a restaurant and a farm and augment them with educational outreach. But once Dan and his brother David (who is Blue Hill's president) got on board, they began to enlarge those original ideas. They wanted to establish a restaurant with the same quality as the original Blue Hill, and they wanted the farming, eating, and education to happen all in the same place. Today, the Rockefeller's seventy-year-old barn has become a modern restaurant kitchen in which composting is a daily activity. As Dan has told interviewers, he wants to make the operation a truly sustainable round trip: "farm to table" and "back to soil." Meanwhile, he wants visitors to see every step of the kitchen process, which is clearly visible through its large windows. After all, nothing's more educational than complete transparency!

Dan's flexible menu relies on seasonal ingredients such as wild ramps and fiddlehead ferns. His intention is to create meals that will help diners understand the close connection between what they're eating and where it comes from. And people are eager to learn. A former hay barn is now part of the Stone Barns education center. The atmosphere is unpretentious and welcoming; the idea is to make even hikers from the nearby state park feel glad to drop in. The plan seems to be working. During my latest visit, on a Thursday afternoon, the parking lot was full; and groups of excited school kids roamed everywhere. (For emerging young gastronomes, Stone Barns Center even offers a summer farm camp.)

Dan's message is as clear as the view from the restaurant to the chicken coops: your experience at Blue Hill at Stone Barns and Stone Barns Center is meant to be shared. The place is easygoing and unpretentious enough for a family visit but also offers a convivial and upscale setting for a special dinner. Now add in the commitment to quality cuisine, and you realize that gastronomy has never had a better setting.

The Proof Is in the Menu

I understand the daily pressures of running a restaurant (chatting isn't part of the job description), so I kept my visit with Dan brisk. We did, however, spend some time commiserating over the pressures of creating a menu from strictly homegrown products. At Blue Hill at Stone Barns, Dan and his team are committed to using seasonal foods grown on the premises or on surrounding Hudson Valley farms, at least as much as possible. As restaurant owners, we have to find the sweet

Sign for the Stone Barns Center
Photo by Jim Weaver

spot that allows us to keep our businesses viable and our customers content—all the while remaining true to Slow Food principles. It's not an easy balance.

Dan and I also talked about the issue of control. Clearly, its effects are felt in the kitchen. "If you can train your cooks to properly truss a chicken," he pointed out, "and if you can control the time it is cooked, the temperature of the oven, et cetera, you can make better chicken—consistently." But, he added, "If you can control the *environment* which the products come from, that's even better." That's the goal at Stone Barns.

Dan told me, "It became clear to me that the obsession with control starts long before the food gets into my hands. Decisions get made before we get the food. So the question becomes 'if you want to be the best-possible chef, how do you get the best food and the best canvas to work with?' It is important to have a relationship with the farmer because that makes it easier." He went on: "Because I want to be a great flavorist, I automatically must become a nutritionist and environmentalist because of conscious decisions about the food that I buy and cook. The best carrot needs to be grown in the best-possible environment. Only then will it have the flavor and vibrancy of what a truly great carrot can be."

Some people in the food business complain that high-profile leaders in the industry have access to the best ingredients simply because of their reputation. I asked Dan about that concern. "I can't blame them," he answered. "I even say that to myself sometimes. But we do pay fair market value for everything that we use from the farm. Sure, it just makes sense that I have first dibs on it all. But the farmers and producers have plenty of people to sell to. And they do."

Many people—including me—have mistakenly assumed that Dan Barber is the one who gets to decide what is grown at Stone Barns. In fact, just the opposite is true. "I am actually *un*-instrumental in what gets grown," he said. "The farmers decide what does best financially, ecologically, and biologically. There is a dance going on, but it's the farmers who lead."

Dan's results, at both Blue Hill at Stone Barns and Blue Hill in New York City, prove that great food doesn't have come with an elitist label. Like the Slow Food philosophy, his menu is approachable, friendly, and accessible. As I read in a *New York* magazine review, Blue Hill "may be the best low-profile restaurant in town." Once you open yourself up to an eating experience there, it literally can change the way you think about—and use—food. People have become so inspired by the authentic, fresh flavors they've discovered at the Barber family's enterprises that they've taken steps to become more involved with the food they eat at home, whether that means planting a windowsill herb garden or becoming an active member of Stone Barns Center. Others have convinced their family and friends to become eager supporters of farmers' markets. Still others have been moved to eat healthier foods, become more physically fit, and spend more time in their own kitchens creating memorable dinners from seasonal foods. There are a million ways to replicate the experience at Blue Hill at Stone Barns. And far from worrying about the competition, Dan Barber and his team urge you to expand on that experience in your own way and in your own neighborhood. That's the legacy they want to carry on to future generations.

✧

Following are a few of Dan Barber's recipes, which he serves at both Blue Hill and Blue Hill at Stone Barns.

Dairyless Fennel Soup

Serves 4–6

3 tbsp. extra-virgin olive oil
1 onion, finely chopped
3 small shallots, peeled and minced
3½ cups diced fennel, white part only, reserving green fronds for garnish
1 apple, peeled, cored, and diced
Sea salt
Freshly ground black pepper
1 tbsp. fennel seeds, crushed
4 cups vegetable stock
½ tsp. chopped thyme

Over a low flame, heat 1 tbsp. of olive oil in a large saucepan, add the onion and shallots, and cook slowly until translucent. Add the fennel and apple, and season with salt and pepper. Cook for a few minutes. Then add the fennel seeds and stock. Increase the heat to medium-high and bring the soup to a boil. Reduce heat to low, and simmer for 30 minutes. Add thyme and season to taste with salt and pepper.

Transfer the soup to a blender and purée, adding the remaining 2 tbsp. olive oil. Return to saucepan and reheat gently. Garnish each serving with fennel fronds.

Kale Salad with Pine Nuts, Currants, and Parmesan

Serves 6 to 8

2 tbsp. dried currants
7 tbsp. white balsamic vinegar
1 tbsp. unseasoned rice vinegar
1 tbsp. honey
1 tbsp. extra-virgin olive oil
1 tsp. sea salt
2 bunches Tuscan kale (about 1 pound), center ribs
   and stems removed, leaves thinly sliced crosswise
2 tbsp. pine nuts, lightly toasted
Parmesan cheese shavings

Place currants in small bowl, and add 5 tbsp. white balsamic vinegar. Let soak overnight. Drain well before use.

In a large bowl, whisk the remaining 2 tbsp. white balsamic vinegar with the rice vinegar, honey, oil, and salt. Add the kale, currants, and pine nuts; toss to coat. Let marinate 20 minutes at room temperature, tossing occasionally. Season to taste with salt and pepper. Sprinkle cheese shavings over salad, and serve.

Cantaloupe Shots with Coppa

Serves 4

1 cantaloupe
Sea salt
Freshly ground black pepper
4 small thin slices of coppa or prosciutto

Preheat oven to 425 degrees.

Cut the cantaloupe in half and remove the seeds. Score the cut side of each cantaloupe half with a knife. Place the halves on a baking tray, cut side up, and bake until the cantaloupe is caramelized, almost black—approximately 25 minutes.

Remove the cantaloupe from the oven, and scoop the flesh into a food processor. Briefly pulse. Season to taste with salt and pepper.

Line a colander with 3 layers of cheesecloth, and set it over a bowl. Scrape the cantaloupe into the colander, and let it drain in the refrigerator overnight. Discard the flesh, and reserve the drained liquid.

To serve, pour the cantaloupe liquid into shot glasses and garnish with piece of coppa or prosciutto.

✄ RESOURCES

Stone Barns Center for Food and Agriculture
630 Bedford Road
Pocantico Hills, NY 10591
(914) 366–6200
http://www.stonebarnscenter.org

Blue Hill at Stone Barns
630 Bedford Road
Pocantico Hills, NY 10591
(914) 366–9600

Blue Hill Restaurant
75 Washington Place
New York, NY 10011
(212) 539–1776

You can learn more about all the Blue Hill enterprises here:

http://www.bluehillfarm.com

14

Going Local and Digging In

When it comes to the food business, somebody is always on the move. Around the world, food is constantly being shunted from one place to the other. Local distributors are up before dawn, busily loading their trucks. Chefs and their teams arrive in the kitchen long before the maitre d' greets the first guests, and they are there long after the last guests have placed their orders.

The growth of the farm-to-table movement has been wonderful for all of us, but there's no doubt that it's added to the complexity of what we do. Whereas mass producers have refined their system to mechanical efficiency, our system is still time-consuming and individualized. That's because each participating farm and restaurant is a crucial part of the whole, meaning that each member needs to have a one-on-one relationship with the others. The details are never-ending. Does a certain farmer need to change her delivery times? Does your restaurant need to triple next week's shipment of arugula and Delaware Bay oysters for a huge society wedding? Do you happen to know of a Slow Food representative who can come to our high school and talk to our twelfth graders about the movement?

The rhythm is different in the mass food industry, which is geared to automated efficiency. Each participant is a small part of the whole picture. Your contribution may be working in the factory, the corporate office, or marketing and sales. Perhaps you're the supplier of the emulsifier components that make the processed cheese last longer. The point is, whether your job is at company headquarters wearing a suit or in a factory wearing a hygienic hairnet, you don't have a view of the big picture, but you aren't expected to, either.

The Slow Food movement is different: we *are* the big picture! We're not just building a sustainable, local system of agriculture; we're rebuilding a community. That means we all have to step in and contribute wherever there's a need. The crux of the challenge is to get everybody talking together: chefs, farmers, truckers, and the many other interested parties, including our young people. Think about it: we can create a Slow Food system, but unless there's a demand for its products into the future, it's doomed to wither away. That's why it's so important to make sure that today's youth are part of our community and our conversation.

Network Guy

If you're looking for an example of someone who has spent his working life helping to build a lasting, sustainable, farm-to-table system as well as garnering the support of young people, you'll want to check out New Jersey native Mikey Azzara. Mikey is young and energetic, and his vision far exceeds his years. His footprint on the local food scene is huge because he works hard to make small changes that add up to big ones. Mikey's perspective is unique because he himself has worked as a full-time farmer—not by way of his family but with inspiration from the environmental studies program at Middlebury College in Vermont, where he earned a degree in psychology.

After farming in both the United States and Italy, Mikey became outreach director at the New Jersey chapter of the Northeast Organic Farming Association (NOFA), which serves eight northeastern states and nearly 5,000 farmers, gardeners, and consumers who support sustainable agriculture practices. He saw his post as a way to reach out to farmers, chefs, and young people. But he wanted to go a step further, so he started his own business, Zone 7. According to his website, Zone 7 is "named after [New Jersey's USDA-designated] growing zone, [and] we source the highest quality ingredients from organic and sustainable farmers in New Jersey and Eastern Pennsylvania and deliver weekly to restaurants and grocery stores."

Even before he started Zone 7, Mikey had been involved with our Slow Food Central New Jersey chapter, and he continues to work with us on many projects and events. One of his big passions is educating local school kids about building a system of sustainable agriculture. "Focusing on a local scale keeps me optimistic because I see positive change every day," he wrote on Chef Ann Cooper's website. "Seeing the excitement of elementary school students this morning while cutting basil at our school garden and making pesto and serving it in the cafeteria. . . . I have no doubt we are on our way. The great thing is that parents and teachers see it too! The kids are telling them at home that the salad's not as good as Mr. Mikey's. Talk about building a demand for fresh foods."

Mikey says that his stint in Italy is what inspired him to come home to New Jersey and promote sustainable agriculture. He explained, "Did I have to go to Italy to learn about organic farming? No. But if you ask if I went to Italy to learn

Mikey Azzara working at the Lawrenceville Elementary School garden
Photo by Jim Weaver

about the values of food, farming, and family, the answer is yes. Good food is a way of life there. Sure, just like here, they're also combating the globalization of food, blah, blah, blah, but they are resisting. Small farms are important there. They may not call it organic farming; it's the way they've been farming for hundreds of years, not because it's a new trendy thing but because it makes sense: rotate the crops and eat the food you've just harvested."

When Mikey returned from Italy to his hometown of Lawrenceville, he discovered that a new business had opened while he'd been gone. "What are the chances of this?" he said. "I come back, and there's an organic farm in my hometown." He was reminded of some advice he got from an Italian farmer before he left: "If you know what you want to do, go after it, and you will be happy." But to develop a local system so that sustainable agriculture can flourish? That was a huge challenge. Luckily, Mikey had plenty of inspiration to fall back on. One of his big influences has been poet and environmental activist Gary Snyder. Writing on Ann Cooper's blog, he explained how Snyder's insights have helped him: "I truly believe that we must all (as Gary Snyder says) 'pick a place and dig in.' A phrase that I now use is, 'Look around and get to work.' Or even better, 'It all starts here.' As a psychology major with a focus on environmental behavior change, I know that this makes sense also because social norms in a community are one of the most influential factors in changing our behavior."

The place Mikey picked to dig in was Lawrenceville. "For starters, people know me here," he wrote. "The principal at the high school is my 6th grade art teacher. The director of the Neighborhood Center is my old baseball coach. They trust me and they are open to my new/old ideas regarding food. And I know *them*. As many of us know, understanding the population and its problems is the key to finding the right solutions."

Getting Everybody Together

Although creating a local network doesn't happen overnight, Mikey's efforts have shown quick results: "When I was at NOFA, that very first spring, I was given permission to launch farmer-chef meetings. At the first meeting, there were seven farmers and chefs who wanted to start doing business together. The next year, there were seventy! All these people started coming together. We did something like speed dating. Each farmer would have two minutes with each chef."

Mikey had invited me to speak at his first farmer-chef meeting because he saw me as someone who was leading the Slow Food charge. He hoped I could help the farmers understand how the movement could enhance their businesses and create a sustainable system of agriculture that would benefit us all. But back then, before a full, humming farm-to-table network was in place, the producers had to be convinced that the idea was cost-effective. Otherwise, they couldn't afford to participate, at least not on a long-range basis.

Whether we're talking about classic cheeses or Rutgers tomatoes, Bourbon Red turkeys or Cape May Salt oysters, quality products require everyone's commitment: from farmers, to delivery people, to restaurant owners. It was my job to show farmers and producers that there is a market for these quality products and that restaurant owners could offer a reliable way to get them from the fields onto our menus. I could have talked until I was blue-faced about the wisdom and rightness of a food system based on fresh, local, seasonal products, but I knew that the only way really to convince the farmers was to *show* them that it could work. The solution I hit on was deceptively simple: throw a party! Our new Slow Food team began to host the first of many food and wine festivals at Tre Piani. We invited the farmers who produced the products to stand alongside the chefs who were alchemizing those products into delicious, fresh, seasonal, locally produced morsels.

Needless to say, the public clamored for more. By bringing supply and demand together, we were able to show everybody involved in the food chain that there is value in supporting the Slow Food movement.

The Key to Success: Distribution

As Mikey honed the relationship between farmers and chefs, he noticed that farmers still "weren't reaching out to chefs directly." That's because one important link was still faulty: distribution. Finally, a chef friend told him, "Dude, just get a truck and start doing this!" After a farmer friend loaned him a refrigerated box truck, Mikey found himself embarking on a new adventure—the very same adventure that Patrick Martins and I had embarked on in our meat distribution scheme (see chapter 8). His one-man distribution system spanned the Garden State and eastern Pennsylvania, and within a month he got a huge boost of encouragement from friends who had been selling to Philadelphia-area restaurants for twenty-five years. They confirmed that distribution had been the missing link, and they encouraged Mikey to keep at it. As I told him, "it needs to happen, and you're the person to do it."

If you want to bring more supporters into a movement, you have to strike a delicate balance. If you come on too strong, you alienate potential members. If you come on too tentatively, people shrug you off. In the Slow Food movement, our challenge hasn't been to convince people that authentic, fresh food, locally grown, is good. The challenge is convincing people that it's worth the extra effort, the extra step, to become part of the system. But you can't browbeat people into taking this step, and that includes not only the consumers but also the people who make a living in the food business. They need to be convinced that paying somewhat more for organic foods and higher-quality breeds is important. They also need to be persuaded to change longstanding work routines as they adjust to dealing more closely with new colleagues. They need to believe in the value of offering foods only in season and be ready for flak from customers who have come to expect that every food should be available year round.

Mikey Azzara's solution to these challenges is simple: he doesn't push. "I'm not big on convincing people," he said. "I guess that's the psychology major in me. We can build this movement from the inside out, focusing on delicious food. After two years of running Zone 7, I can see who's really interested. I don't have time for those who aren't." His strategy is to keep his ear to the ground and learn who in the business might be interested in joining our community. "I've reached out only to farmers and chefs I felt to be the best fit," he said. "I haven't had to make one cold call."

Mikey's full-time work as a farmer has made him sensitive to their concerns. Change is hard, and many are wary of moving to organic farming or getting involved in a local food-distribution network. After all, the corporate food industry has served them well for years, and a standardized system offers a level of security. "I know farmers and the level of trust they need to see before they talk to you," he said. "I can talk to farmers and I can talk to chefs. One of my brothers is a chef. And I worked in restaurants, grocery stores, et cetera, before I was in farming. Besides, I have an outgoing personality and I like to talk on phone. I'm able to bridge the gap."

"My new goal is to help the people who want local, sustainable ingredients. That's where I start. If they're getting what they need from us, and they're running a successful restaurant business, then they tell their friends." He approaches wary farmers like this: " 'Would it be of interest to you to sell some of your stuff to us? If we can take your early wheat harvest on Monday or Tuesday, would that be of interest to you?' These are five-minute conversations. If it doesn't make sense for farmers, they're not going to do it." He added, "There's no way to replace the relationship I have with them. If farmers don't trust you, it's going to be a hard sell no matter how you sell it . . . and of course we would always pay them a fair price."

The soft sell has worked. By spring 2010, after two years in business, Zone 7 had earned the support of twenty-seven participating farms and thirty-three restaurants in New Jersey and eastern Pennsylvania. Both farmers and restaurant owners have been enthusiastic. In a testimonial that appears on the company's website, Tricia Borneman of Blooming Glen Farm in Bucks County, Pennsylvania, wrote, "We love to grow vegetables, and what we grow is gorgeous and delicious— but if we can't sell it all—what's the point?! That's where Zone 7 comes in. The process couldn't be any easier—they're professional, well-connected, young, and energetic, and they're grass roots. They take care of the selling, so we can keep growing! Seriously—we love those guys! Zone 7 is a crucial component of our farm's success, and we look forward to doing business with them for many growing seasons." Scott Anderson, executive chef of Elements, a restaurant in Princeton, New Jersey, contributed this testimonial: "Zone 7 delivers the freshest local produce from quality farms to chefs like us. . . . it's a win-win situation! When we opened, we knew that we wanted to source . . . ingredients from local, sustainable farmers. Seriously, even with a good network of farmers, we could not do what we do without Zone 7."

Out of the Sandbox and into the Dirt

One of Mikey's long-term goals is to get a garden program into every school in New Jersey. His first step is a twist of the "show and tell" concept: he brings farmers and their produce into the schools to talk to the kids. Mikey gets excited when he describes how urban kids pepper the farmers with questions. They overflow with curiosity about a way of life that many of them never knew existed, and they're excited about sampling the food. In an interview posted on YouTube, Mikey described one school presentation: "Bob Muth brought peppers and tomatoes, and Kelly Harding brought some ground beef for hamburgers." But this wasn't just any ground beef: "We got the kids eating these tiny little hamburgers made from grass-fed meat while listening to the farmers talk." As the kids chowed down on the fresh and tasty hamburgers, they were also learning that, because "the cows are eating grass—and everything that comes from the earth—you are, in a sense, eating the grass the cows ate." The goal is to excite the kids so that their generation can keep sustainable agriculture and the philosophy of Slow Food alive. Maybe some of them will even become farmers, like Mikey did. As he says, "I want to take that energy around, and make it happen."

ᴣᴦ

Following is one of the recipes I make at Tre Piani using products that Zone 7 brings me directly from local farms.

Ricotta Gnocchi with Roasted Eggplant, Roasted Peppers, and Mint

Serves 4

GNOCCHI:
I cup sheep's milk ricotta
(drain any excess liquid)
I cup all-purpose flour
¼ cup grated Parmesan cheese
2 eggs
2 tbsp. melted butter

VEGETABLES:
I large eggplant, peeled and cubed (about 2 cups)
I yellow pepper
I red pepper
2 cloves garlic
½ tsp. crushed red pepper
½ cup extra-virgin olive oil
½ cup sheep's milk ricotta
¼ cup chopped fresh mint
Sea salt
Freshly ground black pepper
A few whole mint leaves for garnish

MIXING THE GNOCCHI: Combine all ingredients in an electric mixer with a paddle attachment, or mix them in a bowl by hand until just barely incorporated. Wrap the dough in plastic wrap and let it sit for at least 20 minutes.

Roll the dough into long rods that are about twice as thick as a pencil. Cut each rod into bite-sized pieces, and set the pieces aside in a single layer until ready to use. Keep them cool. You can also freeze them on a cookie sheet in a single layer, and then store them in a plastic bag or freezer container until ready to use.

PREPARING THE VEGETABLES: Preheat your oven to 400 degrees. Place the diced eggplant on a lightly oiled cookie sheet, and roast the pieces until they are soft and beginning to brown around the edges. Remove them and let them cool.

Roast the peppers whole, either on a grill or over the burner of a gas stove until they are soft, look pretty, and are not completely burned. For this dish I like to leave the skin on because it adds good color and a slightly smoky essence. But if the peppers do burn, you can let them cool and completely peel off the skin. Cut the peppers into bite-size squares, being careful not to let the seeds get into the mix.

Slice the garlic thinly.

TO FINISH THE DISH: Bring a large pot of lightly salted water to a boil. Add all the gnocchi. When the gnocchi float, they are done. Remove them with a slotted spoon, and keep them warm.

In a large skillet, heat the olive oil over a medium flame, and add the sliced garlic. Cook until golden brown. Add the crushed red pepper. Add the roasted eggplant and peppers. Cook for 2 minutes until the vegetables are heated through and the oil is evenly distributed. (If the mixture seems a little dry, add more oil. Eggplant tends to soak up oil.) Add the mint and stir thoroughly.

Toss the warm vegetable mix with the hot gnocchi. Season to taste, and serve immediately with the remaining ricotta cheese sprinkled over the top. Garnish with fresh mint leaves.

ᔐ RESOURCES

You can learn more about Mikey Azzara's distribution network here:

Zone 7
http://www.freshfromzone7.com

15

The Brothers Moon
and the Bent Spoon

Will Mooney's stars aligned when he was a kid of fourteen hawking fresh local produce from a farm stand in Cranbury, New Jersey. By the early 1980s, when young Will was plying his roadside trade, an entire generation of Americans had grown up relying on efficient but impersonal supermarket chains for most of their daily food. Most people were satisfied to pluck cucumbers from a bin rather than the ground and to eat restaurant salads with iffy pedigrees. As Will says, "they didn't even realize it wasn't grown around here."

But Will's time was coming. Twenty years after he started selling fresh local produce, Will and his brother Sean opened a restaurant, the Brothers Moon. Today, the restaurant (which he now owns with his wife, Beth Ann) is a big supporter of the seasonal menu concept. And though it will always be hard to convince some diners that asparagus isn't grown year round, the idea of fresh food in season continues to delight customers. Will's known that for a long time—ever since the days he watched motorists screech to a halt on a dusty country road to buy locally grown beans and tomatoes from a New Jersey teenager. That was the Garden State at its best.

But Will's not the only local restaurant owner with that classic image of the Garden State on his mind. It's also been on the mind of Gabrielle Carbone, a special education and psychology major turned serious foodie, who graduated from the French Culinary Institute in New York. In the mid-2000s, Gab and her partner, Matthew Errico, opened the Bent Spoon, an ice-cream shop. "Everything is made from scratch," she told me. "It's a really great thing that seven months out of the year we can make ice cream using ingredients we buy from farmers we know."

Both Will and Gab run businesses that are totally geared to using seasonal, fresh foods from nearby farms and producers. Their success just goes to prove that, when given a choice (and even if it costs a bit more), the public is gravitating to food that, as one of my friends has put it, comes from an address you actually

Chef Will Mooney
Photo by Jim Weaver

recognize. Will and Gab are also very much involved in the Princeton-area Slow Food movement. Yet to appreciate how important it was for these two entrepreneurs to create businesses dedicated to food that's good, clean, and fair, you need to step back and remember the kind of world they are trying to shake off.

In the 1970s, when Will was barely a teenager and Gab still a toddler, mass production looked like it had won the food wars. The standard for high quality meant that food had to withstand cross-country trips, stay as well preserved as a hockey puck, and be as colorful as a neon sign. Yet even in the heyday of mass food production, people were beginning to suspect something was being lost. Nutrition? Flavor? Varieties? Thank goodness the pendulum has swung back to fresh, local fare. Today, Chef Will Mooney is working with meat from pigs that lived happily just over the Pennsylvania border, and Gab and Matt are sending their employees (affectionately known as spoonies) into local strawberry patches to pick the core ingredient for their strictly seasonal ice cream.

The Go-To Guys

Will and I met in New Brunswick, New Jersey, in the late 1980s, when he was cooking at the Frog and the Peach and I was the chef at Panico's. Technically, we were competing with each other (our restaurants were a few blocks apart), but that didn't keep us from becoming friends. Not until later did we find out we were totally in sync with the idea of the Slow Food movement.

Will had an unusual background for the food business. His father is actor, writer, director, and professional storyteller Bill Mooney, and his mother, Valerie Goodall, was an opera star. This is why Will celebrated his first three birthdays in Europe. How do you make the leap from stage and screen to the restaurant business? According to Will, "it's another version of the arts!"

By the time we'd opened our own restaurants, we'd both fully signed on to the whole idea of Slow Food and its commitment to community. For instance, we've been very involved in putting on benefits for child-hunger campaigns. "That's where we share our strengths," Will likes to say. "We're like the team cheerleaders, getting other restaurants involved." As owners of two of the area's original Slow Food–inspired restaurants, we share a bond; and for that reason, we often get yanked into the limelight (which can be both good and bad). In Will's words, "we're the go-to guys for Slow Food!"

We've also come to appreciate the economics of Slow Food. Yes, as a general rule, restaurants pay less for foods that are mass-produced and distributed, even though you'd think that buying food from a farm down the road would be the bargain. But the efficiencies of mass production are what allow these corporations to thrive; and as competitors, local farms face awesome challenges. Their land costs are sky-high, as are the expenses of cutting-edge production and growing techniques. They are transporting in smaller increments, so those costs tend to be higher per unit. It's the same dynamic that drove out the mom-and-pop grocery stores and the high-quality, family-owned dress shops that were once the pride of every Main Street. Local farmers simply can't compete with the sleek efficiencies of supermarkets.

Today the dynamic is shifting again, and both Will and I think going Slow makes good business sense, even if it costs a bit more to begin with. "I think it pays off in the end," Will told me. "I don't think it costs that much more money,

Outside the Brothers Moon Restaurant

Photo by Jim Weaver

and if I'm buying something local, I'm getting a better, fresher product. It's something I can promote, too. Sure, food costs might go up a little bit, but if I have ties with local farms, I can use that fact in my advertising and e-mailing. If I wanted to nitpick, I could say that 'buying local and fresh' can be seen as a marketing expense."

We've both found that using the best, freshest ingredients is a big draw for both the public and professional food lovers. "Food writers love it in this area," Will chuckled. He noted that restaurants that use fresh, locally grown ingredients seem to get more media attention; they are seen as more interesting and cutting-edge. What does it say about our world that simply using fresh, locally grown ingredients can cause such a stir? But, then again, why would a food writer *want* to review the latest fast-food restaurant in her neighborhood?

Going Slow and Seasonal

Will is very fond of Pennsylvania pigs. He brings them to the food and wine festival I host in the summer, and he often features them on the menu at the Brothers

Moon. On a lazy summer afternoon at the food festival, you should see people's faces light up as they sample Will's slow-roasted, pulled pork slathered in his own spice rub and barbecue sauce. Why care about your pigs' pedigree? "Because these pigs are delicious," Will said. They taste so good because they travel only ten miles to get to his restaurant. By contrast, travel-worn pigs tend to taste, well, travel-worn.

When I watch barbecue cook-offs on television or in person, I often wonder why the contestants spend so much time and energy on the special sauces and rigs but don't pay attention to what kind of pig they're working with. Which comes first, the pig or the sauce? I know Will's answer to that question. "Our pigs haven't traveled very far, and I think they are treated very well at the small family farms which we like to support," he told me. "Because they haven't traveled all over the place, we're not spending as much on gas or diesel to get the product." Mass transportation has really screwed up people's instinct for seasonal foods. People are so conditioned to get every food at every time of the year that it's often hard for restaurants to stick to a seasonal menu. As Will pointed out, "we can get green beans cheaper from Guatemala than from right down the street, and that plays into what chefs put on their menus. Year round, people want their green beans and asparagus."

Still, we Slow Food guys keep trying to gently educate our customers. During the height of fresh-food season—roughly from the end of April through October—Will tries to keep about 80 percent of the food on his menu local, which he defines as grown within a twenty-five-mile radius of the Brothers Moon. He works with whatever nature makes available: say, wild leeks, royal mushrooms, fava beans, and asparagus. "A seasonal menu doesn't change the way we cook. It influences *what* we cook. When we're working with local farms, we're getting the food a day or two, maybe three days old, as opposed to when we get it from Central America, Florida, or Texas, when we know it's three, four, or five days old."

He continued: "The fresher the food, the more options you have. Take lettuce, for example. If I get it from a farm that's three or four miles away, even though it costs a little more, I can buy less because I'm using less: the lettuce is fresher; the leaves are standing up. When you buy lettuce from a large store, it's more wilted and a little less happy." The verdict, across the board, is better-tasting food. Fresh carrots? "Vastly different in color, flavor, and scent when they're fresh out of the ground," Will said. Locally made butter? "Did you know that butter in the spring can take on an oniony flavor because of the grass and onions coming through the ground?" It's the way eating used to be: "Local farms aren't trying to harvest as much as they can out of every acre. They're doing it out of pride to get a beautiful potato or carrot, so they end up with a better product."

So can a business be competitive and be a success by going local? "I like to think there's a competitive advantage," Will said, "but I'm not sure there is, though I believe in it. I just don't know if there's a large customer base for eating strictly local foods and whether it's a large driving force behind where people pick and choose to eat. . . . Personally, I like to know where all my food comes from. I like to know the farmer, and know that I kicked the dirt with him. As long as we can develop that kind of relationship with farms, I think we can justify the price."

The Ice-Cream Maker in the Living Room

Gab is easy to like. A bundle of energy, she could be the poster child for Slow Food. When she is not delivering her ice cream around town on the back of her Vespa, she is usually hard at work flitting around her shop. Fiercely independent but as sweet as sorbet, Gab is a staunch supporter of all things Slow Food. "Gosh, I got my first ice-cream maker from my sister when I was fourteen," Gab recalled. "So I had cultivated the idea of fresh ice cream: that it's really good the fresher it is. Probably three or four years before we opened the store, I kept the ice-cream machine in the living room. We'd invite people over and turn it on—and in thirty minutes we had ice cream!"

Clearly, an idea was percolating. Gab and her partner, Matthew, shared an interest in food, though he had a history degree and, at the time, her only degrees were in special education and psychology. In college Gab had joined a Slow Food chapter: "I was just attracted to it." She has also been a longtime admirer of Alice Waters. Nonetheless, it took a while for the pair to figure out their next move. "In retrospect, we were so naïve," she said. "We sort of knew what we wanted to do in our own business, but at first we weren't positive what it was. I had waited tables forever, and Matt was managing a coffee business, where he had become a master barista, a job that requires great craftsmanship. It was such an important thing in his culinary development."

Eventually they figured out that their destiny was to churn world-class ice cream. The Bent Spoon opened in the mid-2000s, its name inspired by the film *The Matrix*, with its mind-bending image of spoons. "It was just so cool," Gab said. From the get-go, Gab and Matt were determined to do business in the Slow Food model. Their ingredients would be fresh, local, and seasonal. They were off and running, and having fun: "I cracked eggs . . . and if we wanted to use rosemary,

Gabby making peach puree at the Bent Spoon

Photo by Jim Weaver

we used rosemary." Unless you're a customer of the Bent Spoon, you might not guess what a terrific ice cream can be made out of herbs. Every spring, Gab says, "It's just about time to be doing herb ice cream!" It's fun to listen to her spring herb litany, with a few side comments thrown in: "There's thyme, chocolate rosemary, lemon balm, lemon verbena, rose geranium, cilantro. . . . Cilantro is an interesting one: some people love it; some people hate it. We make Cointreau-cilantro ice cream—you know, with the orange liqueur? It goes *so well* with cilantro." Gab pauses, then laughs: "And that's what kicks off spring here in New Jersey!"

When you go seasonal, each turn of the calendar brings another surprise. As warm weather approaches, the Bent Spoon gets ready for strawberries, blueberries, and rhubarb. In fact, strawberries were what alerted Gab to one of the more vexing issues that surround the support for local, fresh, and organic foods. Namely, what constitutes good organic food? As its marketing potential has taken off, the *organic* label has become less reliable. "A lot of people in the organic movement have been disappointed at how loose the organic standards are," Gab told me. "A lot more people are able to put organic labels on things that my friends who are organic farmers would never allow—like calling foods *organic* that use certain chemicals."

For answers, Gab turned to an important Slow Food lesson: conscious eating: "This is what the Slow Food movement really counts on—conscious eating. You don't just put *anything* in your mouth; you consciously choose to eat foods that are great." Strawberries brought this lesson to the forefront. "When we first opened, I wanted to make strawberry ice cream and do it in strawberry season, not all year long. But I could not find organically grown strawberries to save my life. It was so upsetting. Strawberries are one of those foods that, if you can afford it, you really should go organic. That's because the fruit has such a thin skin that you can taste the chemicals. I just won't eat non-organic strawberries."

Gab advises that, if cost considerations force you to pick and choose your organic produce, strawberries should be at the top of your list. Bananas can be at the bottom, because of their thick skin. But here's where the organic controversy comes into play. "One year we ordered organic strawberries, and they came from China! 'Wait a minute,' I thought. 'This is ridiculous.' And I sent them back." But a lot has changed since then. "Now all restaurants want to use local farms; you know your farmers, you know what they're using on their fields, not to mention that because of shorter distances you're using less fossil fuels."

Blueberries also lend themselves to local support: "We have these big, fat, juicy blueberries—our blueberry season is out of the world here," she said. The Bent Spoon spoonies often head out to pick the blueberries themselves: "It's me and whoever else," Gab said. "It's such an experience to serve blueberry ice cream later in the week and say, 'I picked the blueberries myself!'"

CSA to the Rescue

Like Will Mooney, Gab is enthusiastic about getting involved in the community-supported agriculture (CSA) movement (see chapter 6). She, too, gets many of her local foods from the Honey Brook Organic Farm in Pennington, New Jersey. Members buy shares, which entitle them to pick up fresh, locally grown food weekly or monthly. Gab told me about the first time she took part: "My CSA that year had a beautiful crop of strawberries. I was so excited. Customers would come in, and I would say, 'Try these strawberries!' You'd bite into one, and it was red throughout, with this incredible flavor. . . . So from that very first year I thought, 'Oh my God, I just want to eat fresh strawberries from New Jersey!'"

Then there's the organically grown New Jersey maple syrup. "I just spent a small fortune on seven gallons; now I'll ration it throughout the year," Gab said. "New Jersey maple syrup is delicious! Okay, it's a small output by Vermont stan-

Outside the Bent Spoon
Photo by Jim Weaver

dards. But how special is this: we're near Princeton University, so people come from all over the world, and they stop in our ice-cream shop and have maple syrup ice cream. And it's not from Vermont or Michigan or anywhere else. It's from New Jersey!" Even better, Gab can drive by the actual places that produce the sweet liquid gold. You know you are at Sweet Sourlands Farm (named after the famous Sourlands preserve nearby) when the farm's beautiful, hand-raised red barn with the solar panels comes into view. "As delicious as it is, there's also something intangible about knowing where the maple syrup comes from. I drive by the trees, I can go into the little room where it's boiled off, and I can pick up the gallons myself. That's the intangible thing about it, what makes it unique. It's not a gimmick."

The next step is to convince the public that fresh, locally grown, authentically organic food isn't a gimmick. People in New Jersey still definitely have trust issues. "I think what drives Matt and me craziest is when somebody says, 'Oh, that's a great marketing slogan. Boy, you sure came up with a great angle to make your ice cream different.' But it's not an angle! It's what we value: good ingredients. If you start with something good, it's more likely to turn out good." Now Gab and Matt are seeing local food sources in the unlikeliest of places. "Down the street, about a block away, is a tiny little courtyard where, oh, maybe fifty years ago, somebody planted a pear tree and a grape trellis," Gab said. The owners of the place are often overrun with beautiful Concord grapes, and they have invited Gab and Matt to take as many as they can use. This is the Slow Food philosophy in action: the spirit of conviviality and community, plus the use of a truly local food source.

"Now our most local flavor is just one block away," Gab laughed. "We don't have a lot of grapes, and now we make the most delicious Concord grape ice cream. . . . It's a special flavor. The pears, which come every other year, are used in a sorbet. Each fruit is treated individually. If you like the flavor of pear, a sorbet is the best way to have it. It's just so pure and clean."

Slow Food and a Special Customer

In 2007, the Bent Spoon served up its ice cream to Carlo Petrini himself. He had flown in from Italy to give a talk in Princeton; and while in the area, he wanted to visit establishments that were practicing his Slow Food philosophy. The Bent Spoon was on his itinerary. "We don't watch a lot of TV or care about the celebrity culture," said Gab, "but when Carlo Petrini came into the store, that had a lot of meaning for me. We only have six seats in front of the store, and he came in and sat down and spent an hour and a half with us."

She laughed: "It was almost like a Slow Food convention. Carlo came with his interpreter, five people from Slow Food USA, as well as Gary Giberson and Mikey Azzara. We were making him taste all the flavors, and the special flavor for him that day was honey ice cream. Did I mention I'm also a beekeeper? Anyway, I had great New Jersey honey, and we made ice cream with homemade honey nougats inside the ice cream. . . . I loved the flavor, and I hope he liked it. He said it was his favorite."

Then a woman named Darcy walked in. According to Gab, "Darcy is this incredible woman who tore up her yard to plant vegetables and then let her neighbors graze off of it." She is also the founding creator of the first school garden project in the Princeton public schools. "Anyway, we're sitting there with Carlo Petrini and Darcy comes in the front door wearing overalls, right? And she looks totally like a farmer, and she's carrying this huge bowl of mint for ice cream. It seemed like it was planned.

"'Oh, Darcy,' I said, 'you couldn't have picked a better time—meet Carlo Petrini!' Well, Darcy is a very robust person, but she's also very quiet, and she didn't really want to say anything.

"But then, very quietly, she says to Carlo, 'I only know one phrase in Italian,' and then she says this beautiful Italian phrase which roughly translates as 'We all eat in one voice.'

"I basically started crying. It was like, could this have been planned? It was such a perfect moment. Those are the kinds of community connections that you don't get from ordering mix from a conglomerate."

ᴖ

Following are a few recipes from the Brothers Moon and the Bent Spoon.

Buttermilk Pancakes

Will Mooney, the Brothers Moon Restaurant

Makes 8 small pancakes

¾ cup all-purpose flour
½ tsp. sea salt
1 ounce sugar
½ tsp. baking soda
½ tsp. baking powder
1 cup buttermilk
1 egg
½ ounce melted butter

Combine dry ingredients and sift. Combine wet ingredients. Add wet to dry, but don't overbeat. Ladle 2-ounce portions onto a lightly buttered sauté pan or griddle over medium heat. Only cook a few at a time so as not to crowd the pan. Keep warm in a damp kitchen towel on a pan in a low heated oven. Serve with maple syrup and berries.

Roasted Chicken Risotto

Will Mooney, the Brothers Moon Restaurant

Serves 4

½ medium onion, finely diced	2 cups chicken meat (preferably Griggstown),
2 stalks celery, finely diced	cooked, picked, and bones and skin removed
I carrot, finely diced	Sea salt
¼ cup extra-virgin olive oil	Freshly ground black pepper
I cup Arborio rice	2 tbsp. butter
I bay leaf	½ cup grated Parmesan cheese
2½ cups hot chicken stock	2 tbsp. chopped parsley

In a large, heavy skillet, slowly cook onions, celery, and carrot in olive oil till translucent. Add rice and the bay leaf; stir to coat all. Add a third of the chicken stock. Stir continuously. Add salt and pepper to taste. When liquid has been absorbed, add half the remaining chicken stock. Keep stirring. When liquid has been absorbed, add the remaining chicken stock.

Stir in the chicken meat. Add butter, cheese, and parsley. Adjust seasoning, and serve immediately.

Creamed Spinach

Will Mooney, the Brothers Moon Restaurant

Serves 4–8

I tbsp. extra-virgin olive oil
I tbsp. minced shallots
I2 cups fresh spinach
I cup heavy cream
I pinch grated nutmeg
Sea salt
Freshly ground black pepper

Over a medium flame, heat the olive oil and shallots in a large pan until they sizzle but do not brown. Add the spinach, and let it wilt to half its original volume. Carefully pour in the cream, and bring the mixture to a simmer. Season with nutmeg and salt and pepper to taste. Serve immediately.

Crispy Wonton Wrappers with Berries and White Chocolate Sauce

Will Mooney, the Brothers Moon Restaurant

Serves 6

WHITE CHOCOLATE SAUCE:
¾ cup water
5 ounces sugar
¼ cup corn syrup
9 ounces white chocolate

WONTON WRAPPERS AND BERRIES:
18 square wonton wrappers
1 tbsp. canola oil
1 cup sugar
4 cups mixed berries
2 cups whipped cream

FOR THE WHITE CHOCOLATE SAUCE: Heat water, sugar, and corn syrup in a medium-sized saucepan until they reach a simmer. Meanwhile, in a medium-sized bowl, break the white chocolate into pieces. Pour the hot syrup over the chocolate, and stir until the mixture forms a smooth sauce. (Any leftovers can be held in the refrigerator for a few weeks.)

TO ASSEMBLE THE DESSERT: Preheat your oven to 325 degrees.

Brush the wonton wrappers with canola oil and dust them with a little sugar. Bake the wrappers on a cookie sheet till they are golden brown, about 10 minutes. Transfer them to a rack, and let them cool.

On each serving plate, alternate layers of berries, wontons, and whipped cream. Drizzle with white chocolate sauce. Serve.

Apple Cobbler

Will Mooney, the Brothers Moon Restaurant

Serves 4

CRUMB TOPPING:
1 cup all-purpose flour
1 cup light-brown sugar
¼ pound lightly salted butter,
    cut into small cubes

APPLE MIXTURE:
4 Granny Smith apples
2 tbsp. sugar
1 tsp. ground cinnamon
1 pinch grated nutmeg
¼ tsp. vanilla extract
2 tbsp. all-purpose flour

FOR THE CRUMB TOPPING: Put the flour and sugar into a food processor, and pulse once to combine. Add the butter, and pulse a few times until the texture is like very coarse cornmeal. Refrigerate for at least 1 hour before using.

TO ASSEMBLE THE COBBLER: Preheat your oven to 350 degrees.

Peel, core, and thinly slice the apples. In a large bowl, combine the apples with the sugar, cinnamon, and nutmeg. Let mixture rest for 15 minutes. Then add the vanilla and flour, stirring well.

Divide the mixture among 4 12-ounce baking dishes or 1 2-quart baking dish. Divide the crumb topping over the dishes. Bake for 25 minutes.

———— · · · ————

Lemon Verbena Ice Cream

Gabrielle Carbone and Matthew Errico, the Bent Spoon

Yields 1 quart

1 cup (¾–1 ounce) loosely packed fresh lemon verbena leaves, washed and dried
¾ cup sugar
2 cups hormone-free whole milk
½ tsp. sea salt
1 farm-fresh egg plus 2 egg yolks
1 cup fresh, cold, hormone-free heavy cream (preferably not ultrapasteurized)
1 tbsp. freshly squeezed lemon juice (preferably organic)
1 tbsp. freshly grated lemon zest (preferably organic)

FOR THE LEMON VERBENA SUGAR: Pulse the freshly picked leaves in a food processor with the sugar until they are finely ground. Set aside in a medium-sized bowl.

FOR THE CUSTARD BASE: In a medium-sized, heavy-bottomed saucepan, heat the milk and the salt until hot (about 140 degrees). While the milk is heating, whisk the egg and yolks in a small bowl next to your stovetop. Once the milk is up to temperature, dip a ¼-cup measure into the hot milk and pour that amount over the egg mixture while you are still whisking the eggs. (This sounds trickier than it is. You are essentially warming the eggs so they don't cook when you pour them into the pot. This process is called *tempering*.) Once the eggs have warmed, start whisking the milk in the pot, and pour the egg mixture right in. Don't stop whisking! Raise the temperature to medium-high, and continue to whisk until a thermometer registers about 170 degrees or the mixture begins to thicken and coat the back of a spoon. (Take care; at 180 degrees this mixture will curdle.) Remove the custard from heat, and pour it through a fine strainer into a metal bowl. Let it cool for 5 minutes.

Finishing the base: Pour the cooled custard over the lemon verbena sugar. Then whisk in the cold cream, fresh lemon juice, and fresh lemon rind. Cover and refrigerate overnight.

Freezing the ice cream: Pour the cold base into your ice-cream maker and freeze according to your maker's directions.

Simply Strawberry Sorbet

Gabrielle Carbone and Matthew Errico, the Bent Spoon

Yields 1 pint

¼ cup water (preferably spring water)
½ cup sugar
½ tsp. sea salt
I pound (4 – 4½ cups) freshly picked strawberries (preferably organic),
    rinsed, hulled, and patted dry
I tbsp. freshly squeezed lemon juice (preferably organic)
I farm-fresh egg white (optional)

MAKING SIMPLE SYRUP: In a saucepan combine the water, sugar, and salt. Cook over moderate heat until the sugar and salt have dissolved.

FINISHING THE BASE: Combine the prepared strawberries, lemon juice, and simple syrup in a blender, and blend until smooth. (You may strain the seeds at this point if you prefer a smoother sorbet.) Cover and refrigerate until cold.

FREEZING THE SORBET: Pour the cold base into your ice-cream maker, and freeze according to the maker's directions. When partially frozen, you may add the optional egg white. This helps to stabilize, emulsify, and preserve the texture of the sorbet if you are going to put it into your freezer and eat it over a few days.

ॐ RESOURCES

The Brothers Moon Restaurant
7 West Broadway
Hopewell, NJ 08525
(609) 333–1330
http://www.brothersmoon.com

The Bent Spoon
35 Palmer Square West
Princeton, NJ 08542
(609) 924–2368
http://www.thebentspoon.net

16

Getting Your Hands Dirty

If you don't understand how the words *New Jersey* and *farms* fit into the same sentence, well, clearly you haven't been to the Garden State. Out-of-staters tend to picture us as an urban outpost, a slightly smaller Big Apple that hasn't fallen far from the tree. But here's the truth: yes, we are part of the tri-state metropolitan area, undoubtedly the most influential power center in the world. But New Jersey is also chockfull of some of the sweetest and lushest farmland on the continent.

Likewise, when you think of Princeton, you may picture campus greens. But you ought to be picturing field greens as well. In reality, the Princeton area is a hotbed of small farms, many so close that they don't even harvest their products until they get the order from local restaurants and markets. As chef and owner of one of those local restaurants, I really appreciate how this cooperative effort keeps getting better and better. Every year there seem to be a few more local farm sources and the distribution chain between them and us seems to get a little more organized.

I like to think that Slow Food has had something to do with the forward momentum. For me and my Tre Piani team, watching the movement take hold has been like seeing our favorite kid grow up and do well. Since the late 1990s, we've worked hard to spread the word about local, sustainable agriculture. In those early years, when we first brought customers and farmers together to talk, eat, and get to know each other, our undertaking was still pretty unusual. Now people are really getting it. Most of them want to support local agriculture; they just need to know how to do it. Likewise, producers need to know there is economic support for getting their product to the public. Today the two sides are starting to work well together and, in the process, to revive the small-farm, local agriculture system that used to thrive in this country.

Farms come in all shapes and sizes. There are small family farms, organic farms, and mushroom farms. There are farms that produce feed for cattle,

A beautiful farm landscape worth preserving in the Hudson Valley

Photo by Jim Weaver

grow stone fruit, or harvest sod. Some enterprises concentrate on herbs; some are living-history farms. Other businesses cultivate cranberry bogs or pick-your-own produce. These creative, energy-filled establishments are springing up everywhere—some of them near our largest cities, others tucked away in small communities. What they have in common is that they have carved out their own niches and are thriving.

One of the most interesting enterprises near the Princeton area is Pitspone Farm. Ask owner Mike Brown to describe his business, and he'll reply, "It's my big backyard!" He really means it: Pitspone Farm *is* his backyard. Mike and his family live on a quiet suburban street in Kendall Park, New Jersey. Behind his house, he has about a quarter-acre under cultivation. The name *Pitspone* is derived from a Hebrew word meaning "very small"; and here, from his tiny corner of Mother Earth, Mike supplies a half-dozen restaurants in the Princeton area—including Tre Piani—with the freshest of produce. He drives it himself to our doors, all of which are no more than thirty minutes from his home. So if you happen to see cherry tomatoes, basil, squash blossoms, padrone peppers, or figs on our menus, chances are high we got them from Mike Brown's farm.

Mike likes to joke, "I only sell to restaurants I can't afford to eat at." Though you might not read about this business model in a textbook, it sure works for Mike. He's developed a high-end clientele that can afford to buy his naturally grown and absolutely fresh products. All of them are seasonal, and some of them, like his figs, are an unusual find in New Jersey.

Launched in 2006, Pitspone Farm is literally Mike's summer job. During off-season, he works as a school librarian, and he got inspired to create the farm in a roundabout way. For one thing, "I just like to grow things." For another, he lived in Israel for ten years, where he met his wife, Nurit, and learned to appreciate figs. These Mediterranean delicacies aren't indigenous to New Jersey, but they are growable under skillful hands like Mike's. Once he started growing them he never stopped. Now figs from Pitspone Farm have become a menu staple in local, upscale restaurants and also represent a bit of home for Nurit. "She's my best fig customer, and one of the original reasons I grew them was that she likes them," Mike says. At Tre Piani, we've kept two of Mike's fig trees in giant planters outside our front door for years. Thanks to our wonderful maitre d' Giancarlo, they have somehow survived several harsh winters. (Sometimes I have a feeling that he's the reason Tre Piani thrives too.)

Between raising their three kids, writing a couple of books (including *The Jewish Gardening Cookbook*), and working full time as a librarian, Mike Brown is a great example of a new breed of farmer: one with his hands in the soil and a lot of irons in the fire. At Pitspone Farm, he has the flexibility to experiment with different crop combinations every year. One newcomer is alpine strawberries, a small, aromatic version of the standard variety; and Mike is still deciding whether there's enough demand to make it economically viable to keep growing. But along with flexibility, he's got the responsibility of doing everything himself: "I'm really up against full-time farmers who have hired labor and large areas of land. Here I'm the laborer, the marketer, the owner—I'm everything. And I have to grow a mix of things suited to my situation. For example, I can't grow things like corn that require a lot of acreage. Besides, I don't have the machinery for it."

Whatever he raises, Mike is able to get it to his client restaurants in well under an hour. ("I pick it and get it there.") This means that he can sell to us in small quantities, which eliminates waste and ensures that his produce is the freshest available. Mike says that the income from the farm "gets us through the summer," but clearly this is a labor of love rather than a huge moneymaker. Part of

Front-yard farm in the Hudson Valley

Photo by Jim Weaver

that satisfaction comes from his relationship with a small core of restaurants and chefs. One year he experimented with selling to the public, but that didn't work. For one thing, he found he had to charge, say, eight dollars a pound for padrone peppers, which is much more than most individuals want to pay. But the restaurant trade buys the peppers in larger quantities, which makes more economic sense.

Moreover, many individuals didn't understand that Pitspone Farm isn't a huge commercial enterprise. It's the Browns' home. When customers asked if they could stop by to pick up some produce, he'd tell them, "Please call before you come." Instead, "people would come to the door at all different times." And once they were there, some were so lulled by the relaxed atmosphere of a small family enterprise that they didn't want to leave. Between handholding customers and running a one-man business, this approach to sales "just wasn't a viable model for me." Now he's content to stay with a small, self-contained operation that he can handle himself. Besides, Nurit has her own full-time job and has made it clear that Mike's backyard enterprise better stay where it is. Mike laughs, "I promised her I'd leave the front yard alone."

Talking Turkey

To get a handle on the variety of New Jersey small farms, consider this: Pitspone Farm is strictly a twenty-first-century enterprise, while Lee's Turkey Farm in East Windsor, New Jersey, goes back to 1868. Yet both farms are city-friendly enterprises, though Pitspone Farm is comprised of the Brown's backyard while Lee Turkey Farm fills, as its website says, "54 acres nestled in the arms of suburbia." Pitspone Farm doesn't have a website because Mike Brown works directly with a small group of chefs and doesn't need to advertise to the public. But Lee's Turkey Farm, which has been farmed by six generations of Lees, not only has a website but a lively marketing outreach program.

The Lee farmers of 150 years ago would be startled by the website. What would they make of the rollicking fiddle music that blasts from the homepage or the invitation to the public to stop by and help themselves to the food? "Hundreds of fruit trees and acres of vegetables all yours for the picking," invites the site, "and a market for people on the go looking for the freshest and most tasteful produce. . . . Lee Turkey Farm also holds true to its name raising 5,000 turkeys annually with the highest quality, oven-ready turkeys and turkey parts available year-round."

Proprietor Ronny Lee and his extended family live on the property in two farmhouses. But even though Ronny looks more like a surfer dude than a farmer, rest assured that he's earned his tan and his buff arms from hard outdoor work. One day I drove over to the turkey farm to pay him a visit. I was writing an article about corn; and because Ronny grows a lot of it, I wanted to hear his thoughts. He was nowhere in sight when I pulled into the parking lot, but I could hear his tractor. He was plowing under a small field of cauliflower that had outgrown itself and was no longer fit to eat. The best place for it now was back underground where it could nourish the soil.

When Ronny saw me, he waved and signaled to me to give him a moment while he finished his job. I knew enough to wait patiently. If farmers have a task that needs doing, they finish it before turning to something unproductive, such as a conversation in the middle of the day. But eventually he and his giant tractor rumbled toward me.

"Hey," I said, "thanks for taking the time to talk with me today."

"No problem," Ronny replied. "Always glad to talk about corn. Nobody's corn is sweeter than what we plant right here."

"What variety do you grow?" was my first question.

Ronny sat back on his seat, raised the brim of his hat, and looked down at me good-naturedly for a moment. Then he barked, "I can't tell you that. No farmer will tell you that. All I can tell you is my early varieties are the same as everyone else—Silver Queen, mostly. But my really good corn, the corn that comes later in the season? That's a secret. I won't even tell you the kind of corn I grow to feed my *turkeys*." I never expected to learn so much about farming by not getting an answer.

The Compost Guy

Farmers work with many secret ingredients. One—and arguably the most important—is the soil, which is truly the lifeblood of a farm. Most people do not think about the miracles that happen in fields, gardens, and forests, every day, in every season. But such miracles don't happen without a rich and healthy soil. Have you ever sped down a country road in August and watched the fields of corn wave proudly? It's a majestic sight, a reminder of barbecues, and parties at dusk, and long Labor Day weekends. It's as if that ripe waving corn is singing, "Hey, summer has been great, and all's right with the world!" But it was good soil that produced that good corn.

Soil is a living thing, with its own ecosystem and life-sustaining universe. Sure, to the naked eye, the earth in a field looks static and motionless. Yet actually it's in a perpetual state of growth, nourishment, harvest, and natural decay. Think about it: last year's foliage is plowed under the soil and thus becomes the soil's fertilizer. Various bacteria eat the rotting debris, as do insects and fungi. Beneath the soil's surface, these organisms grow and thrive, building an environment bursting with life and the ability to pass on life. A healthy soil is as rambunctious and unstoppable (and as dirty!) as a healthy four-year-old kid. It's the farmer's job to make the most of that soil. And as I became more involved with local growers, I learned that each farmer's technique is unique, just as each chef's work is unique. Of course, both cooks and farmers rely on tried-and-true techniques and classic recipes to coax forth the food's flavors. But they also have secret methods and ingredients. In the case of soil, those secret ingredients involve compost.

In chapter 13, I introduced you to Stone Barns Center for Food and Agriculture, an innovative, nonprofit, four-season farm and education center set on eighty acres in Pocantico Hills, New York. Gregg Twehues is director of nutrient management at Stone Barns, and his focus is the center's farm, which is a leader in developing a locally based, sustainable approach to agriculture. That goal requires

Ewe Poo compost made by Valley Shepherd Creamery

Photo by Jim Weaver

top-rate soil, and soil is Gregg's job. "When you have the control to make your own compost," he says, "*that's* when you can control quality."

Compost can be defined as "a mixture of decaying organic matter, as from leaves and manure, used to improve soil structure and provide nutrients." Gregg explains that, for a large enterprise such as Stone Barns, controlling compost means being able to block the intrusion of "potential diseases, pathogens, and pesticides" and to nurture material that is "highly enriched with biological activity." Composting is a science; there's a way to do it right. Moreover, it can be a real economic advantage. According to Gregg, "if you start composting in an organized manner you can reduce production costs and labor by as much as 50 percent." But you don't need a big enterprise to take advantage of composting. Today many people routinely make compost at home, which is great. The idea is startlingly simple: instead of discarding food waste, says Gregg, "turn it into the next generation of food!"

The farm at Stone Barns has also been composting the huge number of cardboard boxes that are epidemic at any large business; at Stone Barns this amounts to 800 to 1,000 pounds of cardboard per week. In the past workers shipped the discards to a recycling center, but Gregg says that "we were not comfortable about it because it was still creating a carbon footprint." Today they shred the cardboard and use it in pig bedding, where it breaks down further until it becomes a suitable bulking agent for food-waste composting. In the synergistic process that follows, the farm is able to recover about 65 percent of the food waste in the kitchen.

Our compost discussion could stray into a riff on bacteria and fungi and green manures, but let's just summarize by saying that Gregg Twehues and his perfectly balanced compost program have allowed Stone Barns' farmland to become self-sufficient and healthy without requiring any added chemicals or leaving it susceptible to outside diseases. "What makes us unique is that we're a closed system: we don't take in any outside materials," Gregg says. Furthermore, through the application of the latest agriculture science and good land stewardship, Stone Barns has increased its efficiency and saved costs. Under a traditional system of management, farms and food businesses pay people to haul away used food and waste materials. Stone Barns has become a leader in showing how such discards can be kept on site to sustain and nurture the soil. Not only that, the center has so much prime compost that it now sells it to others: "Before, we were paying people to take this material away. . . . Now we're charging *them.*"

Preserving Paradise

Soil is crucial to developing fresh, wholesome food. So is the land it sits on. That's where the New Jersey Farmland Preservation program comes in. Under this program, which is administered by the state's Agriculture Development Committee, farmers can sell their development easements to approved municipalities or nonprofit entities. The land is still theirs to farm on (it does not become public property); but in exchange for the sale, the owner agrees to use it only for agricultural purposes forever. One of the program's participants is Pegi Ballister-Howells, whom you met in chapter 6. In addition to being one of the region's most knowledgeable food, agriculture, and horticulture experts, Pegi is a farmer: owner and proprietor of Blooming Acres, a ten-acre farm in East Windsor, New Jersey. It's one of the smallest pieces of farmland participating in the New Jersey Farmland Preservation program.

"Getting into the program was tricky because there was a ton of paperwork," Pegi says. "But I have no regrets." Today, nine and a half acres of Blooming Acres is under the preservation program. Although Pegi's farm amounts to just a tiny dot on the planet, it fits the program's criteria because it's contiguous with a large farm

An urban farm behind Roberta's Restaurant in Brooklyn, New York
Photo by Jim Weaver

across the street. Plus, it received high marks for having top-quality soil. Pegi attributes her hearty soil to the fact that Blooming Acres was once part of a potato farm. Potatoes can be notoriously difficult vegetables to grow in New Jersey soil. But out of adversity came strength. Today, the land consists of eighteen inches of top soil sitting on, as Pegi calls it, "a beautiful aquifer . . . perfect farmland!" She adds, "Our soil is considered number one, and it's one of the main reasons we were accepted into the program. We have no wet spots and good drainage."

Pegi is now committed to preserving the land as strictly agricultural. Besides raising goats and chickens, she has a five-and-a-half-acre nursery for growing Christmas trees, which are marketed locally. In addition, she collects "all sorts of weird ornamentals" that appear in her photographs, books, TV and radio shows, and seminars. They include a strange redwood tree (indigenous to China) which should have grown from a seedling into a twenty-foot-tall tree but instead turned "into a round green ball, totally bizarre." Thanks to the New Jersey Farmland Preservation program, Pegi has created "a little horticultural paradise." But of course, for people such as Pegi, Mike Brown, Ronny Lee, and Gregg Twehues, soil and paradise are often one and the same.

ℨ

Following are a couple of simple recipes from Tre Piani.

- - - - - - - - - -

Baked Eggplant and Goat Cheese Fondue

Makes about 2 cups

4 cloves garlic	Sea salt
½ cup extra-virgin olive oil	Freshly ground black pepper
1 large eggplant	¼ cup grated Parmesan, Manchego,
6 ounces fresh goat cheese	or another sharp grating cheese
2 eggs	¼ cup diced fresh tomato
4 leaves basil, julienne-cut	Pita chips

Preheat the oven to 350 degrees. Peel the garlic cloves, leaving them whole. Pour the olive oil into a small, ovenproof pan, add the garlic, and cover with a lid or aluminum foil. Bake for 25 minutes, or until the gloves are soft and golden brown. Remove from oven, and set aside. (You can roast garlic up to a week ahead of time, and you can reuse the oil to season your favorite dish or drizzle over bread, grilled meats, or seafood.)

Slice the eggplant in half lengthwise, place it flesh side down on a lightly oiled pan, and roast until soft, about 30 minutes. Let the eggplant cool to room temperature. Then scoop out the flesh and put it into the bowl of a food processor, discarding the skin. Add the roasted garlic, goat cheese, eggs, salt, pepper, basil, and half of the Parmesan. Pulse in the food processor until the mixture is barely pureed.

Put the pureed mixture into an ovenproof crock, and top it with the diced tomato and the remaining Parmesan. Bake at 350 degrees until the puree is bubbling hot, about 30 minutes. Serve immediately with pita chips to dip.

Pasta Primavera

Serves 4 as an entrée, 8 as an appetizer

½ cup extra-virgin olive oil
4 cloves garlic, peeled and sliced
1 yellow pepper, seeded and julienne-cut
1 red pepper, seeded and julienne-cut
1 carrot, peeled and julienne-cut
½ cup haricots verts (thin French green beans),
    cleaned and cut in half crosswise
½ cup broccoli florets
1 cup peeled, seeded, and diced fresh tomato
1 pound pasta, any shape
1 zucchini, trimmed, cut in half lengthwise, and sliced
½ cup sliced mushrooms
1 bunch spinach, washed, stemmed, and roughly chopped
    (about 2 cups loosely packed)
4 leaves fresh basil
1 tsp. crushed red pepper
Sea salt
Parmesan, Pecorino, Manchego, or feta cheese (optional)

Bring a large pot of lightly salted water to a boil.

In another large pot, preferably heavy gauge, heat the olive oil over a low flame. Add the sliced garlic, and cook until it is golden brown. Add the peppers, carrots, beans, and broccoli. Simmer until the vegetables begin to sweat, about 10 minutes. Add the tomatoes, and cook for another 10 minutes.

When the lightly salted water comes to a boil, add the pasta, and cook according to the manufacturer's instructions.

Meanwhile, add the zucchini, mushrooms, and spinach to the pot of vegetables. Cook for another 5 minutes or so. Add the basil, and season with the red pepper and salt to taste.

Drain the pasta thoroughly, and toss it with the vegetables. Serve immediately, and pass the cheese (grated or crumbled) at the table.

᧿ RESOURCES

Lee Turkey Farm
201 Hickory Corner Road
East Windsor, NJ 08520
(609) 448–0629
http://www.leeturkeyfarm.com

New Jersey Farmland Preservation
http://www.nj.gov/agriculture/sadc/farmpreserve

17

So Where Are We Now?

It used to be that the term *slow food* made people ask, "Are you talking about cooking in a crock pot?" No longer. Today most people understand that we're talking about supporting a food supply that's seasonal and locally grown and based on sustainable agriculture and environmentally sound practices—food that's accountable "from plate to planet." Slow Food USA now comprises more than two hundred chapters, and its membership is growing exponentially. But whether or not people become card-carrying members of our movement, more and more of them are seeking out and supporting the idea of local growers and producers.

In many towns and cities, farmers' markets have become huge, interactive events, just as they were in village squares several centuries ago. Even in the super-market, once-reluctant shoppers are experimenting with seasonal veggies rather than heading straight for frozen meals in boiler bags or on microwavable trays. Others are bypassing the processed cheese that tastes like Play-Doh and training their palates and noses to love the pungent varieties offered by local cheesemakers. Notably, many mass-production food companies now entice consumers with the words *natural* and *hormone-free* on their packaging (though buyers should beware: those words are often used unreliably). People are voting with their pocketbooks, too: they are buying organic food and flocking to businesses that sell food that's whole-grain, wild-caught, and raw.

People are having fun with food again! They're chatting with the neighbors every Saturday at the farmers' market or joining their kids' class tour of a local cheese maker. They're sparking up their Thanksgiving menu with a Heritage Breed turkey, charming their guests with stories about Ben Franklin and that noble bird. Why not spend a few extra dollars once a year to feed your loved ones with the very best? Why not embrace the idea of Slow Food in your own individual way?

With all of this change in the air, I often hear the question "So, what now, Jim? Where is the movement going from here?" Currently, we're seeing four major trends. First, the food movement is growing in political and cultural clout. Although Slow Food USA is a leader in this grassroots awareness effort, a number of other organizations and pressure groups are also dedicated to reforming the country's food network, as Michael Pollan discusses in his article "Food Movement, Rising," which recently appeared in the *New York Review of Books.* Second, there's a push to establish food communities: natural groupings of people with interest in sustainable agriculture and locally produced food, an idea that Carlo Petrini explores in his book *Terra Madre.* Third, Slow Food USA is continuing to monitor and refine the movement's goals as its membership grows. Finally, and perhaps most importantly, many organizations are making concerted efforts to teach the next generation about food issues.

Welcome to the "Big Lumpy Tent"

In his 2010 article, "Food Movement, Rising," Michael Pollan suggests that we have reached a cultural crossroad: "Cheap food has become an indispensable pillar of the modern economy. But it is no longer an invisible or uncontested one. One of the most interesting social movements to emerge in the last few years is the 'food movement,' or perhaps I should say 'movements,' since it is unified as yet by little more than the recognition that industrial food production is in need of reform because its social/environmental/public health/animal welfare/gastronomic costs are too high." Pollan notes that, historically, Americans have been conditioned not to worry about food because it's been so plentiful. We spend less than 10 percent of our incomes on food, less than any other society in history. For that reason, "Americans have not had to think very hard about where their food comes from or what it is doing to the planet, their bodies, and their society." Until very recently, it's also meant that "food in America has been more or less invisible, politically speaking."

But it turns out we've made a devil's bargain. Sure, we eliminated humankind's most basic anxiety—"Will I be hungry tonight?"—but at the expense of altering our food supply through chemistry and mass production. As an example, Pollan cites the "steady stream of more than 17,000 'novel food products,'" made with at least some artificial components, that end up on grocery shelves every year. He warns, however, that reliance on a "cheap food supply" is about to change, thanks to the looming rise in fossil fuel expenses (which will make mass transportation more prohibitive) and growing worries that our food production chain is becoming more vulnerable to contamination.

Wild Hive Store and Café Bakery in Clinton Corners, New York:
a huge supporter of Slow Food

Photo by Jim Weaver

As a result, food advocacy groups, including Slow Food USA, are on the rise; and they are begin to band together under what Pollan calls a "big lumpy tent." He calls it "lumpy" because these causes cut across political lines and touch many sensibilities, sometimes at cross-purposes. They are addressing school lunch reform, animal rights issues, the promotion of organic and locally grown food, the viability of a locally based food culture, food safety, and regulatory issues that affect farmers, food providers, and entrepreneurs. Their approach to these issues will evolve as lobbying and legislation change the food landscape. For now, all we can say is that good food clearly matters to many different kinds of people—from suburban parents to urban activists, from growers to distributors, from restaurant owners to home cooks. We're all in this together.

Local Food Communities: The Return of the Public Square

The idea behind Carlo Petrini's *Terra Madre* is this: eaters and producers must unite to create networks in which local markets, neighborly interdependence, and conviviality can bloom. But as Michael Pollan points out, Carlo's concept doesn't just include people in neighboring zip codes. It also means that well-to-do eaters in the United States should be willing to pay more to help support "nomad fisher folk in Mauritania by creating a market for their bottarga, or dried mullet roe." That's true neighborliness, on a global scale.

For an example closer to home, consider your local farmers' market. Pollan writes that there are now more than 5,000 farmers' markets around the country. At last count there were almost 250 in New Jersey alone, far more than the number in existence a decade ago. Pollan describes a typical farmers' market scene: "Someone is collecting signatures on a petition. Someone else is playing music. Children are everywhere, sampling fresh produce, talking to farmers. Friends and acquaintances stop to chat. One sociologist calculated that people have ten times as many conversations at the farmers' market than they do in the supermarket. . . . In many cities and towns, farmers' markets have taken on (and not for the first time) the function of a lively new public square." Not every town has an actual square, but every town or neighborhood can band together to enjoy truly good food, share conversation with neighbors, and support local and regional producers. This is what has held communities together for as long as we've populated the planet.

The Role of Slow Food USA

It's not false modesty to observe that the Slow Food philosophy has been a leader in galvanizing the public to search for a sense of community that's based on an authentic, seasonal, and locally based food supply. Although Slow Food USA is an offshoot of Slow Food International and inspired by Carlo Petrini's vision, food issues in America diverge widely from those in Italy. The United States is vast, both culturally and geographically, with a mass food system that's equally complex and vast. Italy is much more culturally cohesive, retaining many of its food and farming traditions even as it faces modernization pressures.

Here at Slow Food USA, we can talk earnestly of all the supportive measures we've launched, but let's not forget the simplest and most powerful: educating while mingling has made our mission a lot of fun. Today, the movement's future looks robust. "Public awareness and interest in membership have exploded," says Jerusha Klemperer, the organization's program manager for campaigns and projects. More than 225 Slow Food chapters have sprung up around the country; and President Josh Viertel says that Slow Food USA's mailing list, which doubled in 2009 alone, now surpasses 200,000 recipients. "These are all people that are making change happen," he says. "These are the people that can sign petitions, make phone calls, and vote for changes. Small steps lead to big steps. The goal is to organize all of the local chapters to eventually band together and make huge changes in food policy, regulations, and fixing the farm bill." In his eyes, the role of the national office is "to facilitate local chapters and to come up with ideas and programs that can be integrated on local levels."

So what does the national office think of our Slow Food efforts here in New Jersey? According to Josh, "surprise" is the word that comes to mind. He finds it amazing to consider how many inroads Slow Food has made on the local level. Josh points out that it's the local chapters that are doing the front-line work, where you find the amazing people who dedicate so much of their time to making change happen. He notes, "If you have read Michael Pollan, and his words upset or inspired you, that can result in change. Or maybe you dropped off your child at her first day of school and you worry about the food she and her classmates will eat, and that it's part of the industrial food chain. From that worry, you can move forward and begin to make a difference. Join your local Slow Food chapter and help change your local food policy; start supporting a farmers' market, and vote locally with your food dollars."

Slow Food is sometimes accused of being the refuge of elite foodies. Jerusha Klemperer says she understands why people say this, but she believes the movement is making strides toward its goal of giving everyone access to affordable, sustainable food. "We're not about fancy food," she says. "We're about making food that's good for the people who eat it, good for the people for grow it, and good for the environment. To have that kind of food is the right and privilege of everyone." She goes on to explain, "Slow Food is about empowering individuals and communities to make change." The movement concentrates on grassroots lobbying that educates and inspires consumers and activists of whatever political persuasion. As Michael Pollan points out, that cuts a wide swath: from conservative libertarians who oppose many regulatory structures and embrace local farming as a family-values issue all the way to the political left, where food reform has captured the attention of animal-rights proponents, environmentalists, and social-justice activists. "It is our hope—if we're going to make changes in this food system—that this can be a nonpartisan issue," Klemperer says. "We talk about 'food politics,' but we are partly blind; we want to appeal to people on all parts of the spectrum."

Meanwhile, organizers are working to increase support for the movement one person at a time. Klemperer likens the process to way in which drops of water collect in a sink, until little by little they fill the basin. It's a slow and steady approach, she notes, but "that's where strength comes from." Still, many people wonder if the Slow Food movement will actually be able to reform our food system. Klemperer is quick to answer: "Fast food became a unifying factor in this country. If fast food can do it, so can we!"

The Next Generation

Ultimately, the health of any movement depends on its new blood. That's why education and programs for young people are so important. Slow Food USA is committed to the Youth Food Movement, which launched in 2007 at the University of Gastronomic Sciences in Pollenzo, Italy, an institution dedicated, under Carlo Petrini's leadership, to the "awakening and strengthening of an international network of young farmers, producers, students, chefs, and activists." Michael Pollan notes, "What is attracting so many people to the movement today (and young people in particular) is a much less conventional kind of politics, one that is about something more than food. The food movement is also about community, identity, pleasure, and, most notably, about carving out a new social and economic space removed from the influence of big corporations on the one side and government on the other. "

Earlier in this book I introduced you to Alice Waters, who founded the first school-based, hands-on, get-down-and-dirty gardening program for urban kids. Today, her idea has been replicated in many cities and school districts and has led to the growth of another program, the School Lunch Initiative, which has become a staple in the American public school system. Now an entire generation of kids has learned about the value of a nutritious lunch along with gardening skills. As they've moved into young adulthood, some have been inspired to turn these interests into careers. They started by learning about sustainable agriculture and ended by getting out there to make it happen: now that's a new kind of farm team.

Lani Raider is one of the team's star players. She is a former chapter leader of Slow Food Hudson Valley and until recently was an associate professor at the Culinary Institute of America, where she volunteered as the faculty advisor for the campus agricultural club Chefs Sustaining Agriculture. The name is a deliberate play on the phrase *community-supported agriculture* (CSA), a cooperative food venture that I've discussed throughout this book. For the young people in the campus CSA group, working with Lani was an eye-opener. Many are from cities and suburbs,

Sign for the Culinary Institute of America

Photo by Jim Weaver

and they were studying at the institute to become chefs and managers of restaurants and other food-oriented businesses. Lani's first goal with these students? To shake them up. "My goal was to help confuse them," she says. "Because once they start asking questions, they'll search for answers. My goal was to awaken people out of their numbed stupor, to bring them back to a place where the palate plays a normal role in the food we eat."

To teach this lesson, Lani took her CSA students to the best classroom of all: the farm. "The minute they tasted food from the farm, it changed them forever," she says. "It's so much fresher, so much more delicious. They said, 'Oh, my God, if *that's* what a carrot really tastes like, what about milk and strawberries and asparagus?' It's the difference between food being shipped 1,500 miles and more, and something that's just minutes old. Once people taste the difference, they will drive distances to get these fresh and local products."

Lani says that many students assume that food is always available, so the idea of eating in season is a novel concept: "One student never had a sugar snap pea in her life. She didn't even know how to eat it!" Her students also learned about the realities of farming: "A student will ask a farmer, 'Why is milk seven dollars

The Culinary Institute of America
Photo by Jim Weaver

a gallon?' And then the farmer explains what it means to be an independent in this country as opposed to being part of a company that gets subsidies from the government."

Lani practices what she teaches. Last year, her CSA students put on a harvest dinner with a menu that was 100 percent local, "right down to the vinegar." She says, "The butter and dairy, the coffee (locally roasted by a small fair-trade company), the meat: all was produced locally. The only thing we didn't get locally was the fat, and we're working on that." (For now, they use olive oil from Italy.)

Lani has had an unusual food journey. A native Californian, she was a long-time vegetarian until persistent anemia forced her to find a new way to eat. She discovered that Slow Food gave her a way to track the humane treatment of livestock and natural, authentic food products. Gradually, she reintroduced animal products into her diet and found that there's a world of difference between mass-slaughtered food and the careful, intentional, and humane raising of quality livestock for food. Today, she's even learning to slaughter chickens.

She admits that her food lifestyle is stricter than most people's. Once a week she goes to her local CSA co-op to pick up produce. Whatever is seasonal, fresh, and available, that's what she eats. Period. She makes no supermarket runs at all. "I'm pretty extreme," she says. But waiting for a favorite food to come into season is also part of the fun: "I like waiting for sugar snap peas: that moment when you are eating them, at the moment of perfection—that's worth waiting for. There's this anxiety and excitement, 'Oh, my God, one more week for sugar snap peas!'" She laughs and then explains that her intent isn't to intimidate students into thinking they must do the same: "I'm kind of at the extreme end of the spectrum, but I believe they can start with one ingredient, or one meal. . . . They can try it for a week."

Lani is energized about the future of the sustainable food culture, but she also sees that we have a lot of work to do: "We're so terribly disconnected. People don't realize the possibilities, how food can be connected to them in different ways, and how those connections can keep farmers in their regions when you decide to purchase locally." She points out that today we have two food systems in this country: one a mass-production network that can take advantage of government food subsidies, the other an independent network of local producers who rely on their communities and regions for support. But the independents have a secret weapon that's becoming less of a secret all the time. You might call it the powerful human instinct to band together in communities—in this case, propelled by a force that we cannot deny: we must eat. "Food is the great equalizer," Lani says. "As a country, we're wavering because we're not grounded, but food can be that grounding force, no matter what your religion is or your economic status or your political agenda or the music you listen to or the person you love. Everybody eats!"

She predicts that the grounding force of food will help people and communities connect again and reform our food culture: "That's why, although it's not easy, I think we're going to see a resurgence of food that tastes good, and a new understanding about health and real food. The minute people taste good food, they become rooted in humanity in a different way. Food becomes precious. It's no longer that I want a handful of big strawberries out of a supermarket box. It's that these two little delicious strawberries I just picked off the vine are *enough*. When you understand that, everything shifts. Your connection with the world shifts. It makes you understand that, in so many ways, we can be citizens of the world and think beyond ourselves."

To read Michael Pollan's article, visit:

> http://www.nybooks.com/articles/archives/2010/jun/10/food-movement-rising

To learn more about the University of Gastronomic Sciences in Pollenzo, Italy, visit:

> http://www.unisg.it

18

Conviviality

On a sweet summer night in 2010, I gathered together at Tre Piani many of the people who have joined me in bringing Slow Food to our own corner of the planet. We are local farmers, chefs, food-business owners, educators, and activists. Whatever our calling, we all are doing our part to promote food that's been produced, raised, and prepared in a way that's "good, clean, and fair." That night, the sixteen of us tucked into a banquet that included produce from the Tri-County Auction and Zone 7, chicken from Griggstown Quail Farm, cheese and ham hocks from Cherry Grove Organic Farm, Cape May Salt oysters, and tilefish and tuna from Viking Village. We enjoyed homemade pickles made from cucumbers bought at the Hightstown auction, egg salad made from local eggs, roasted eggplant, and, of course, New Jersey tomatoes. Everything was fortified with hearty wine and beer.

As I looked around the table, I thought about how far Carlo Petrini's original idea had spread. Here we were in New Jersey, all of us preoccupied with carrying on his movement, all of us energized about restoring a food system that doesn't just support local suppliers and farms but truly unites communities. Conviviality is one of the pillars of the Slow Food philosophy; and as my book comes to an end, I think it's only right to quote the movement's official description of its power: "May suitable doses of guaranteed sensual pleasure and slow, long-lasting enjoyment preserve us from the contagion of the multitude who mistake frenzy for efficiency. Our defense should begin at the table with Slow Food."

Those of us who gathered together on that midsummer evening understood that Slow Food can also be seen as a metaphor for quality of life. A good life requires proper nourishment of mind and body. It also needs love: of oneself, of one's friends, of one's family, of one's food. I looked around that table, grateful to be with these friends and proud of what we've accomplished. I recalled that, several years ago, it had dawned on me that we were embarking on a remarkable mission one that was larger than all of us. That's when I knew I needed to write this book.

As I neared the end of this project, Jean Torkelson, the writer who'd helped me put this story into words, suggested that I should throw a dinner party for the people I'd been writing about. It would be a way to give them a chance to talk about what the movement means to each of them. Hey, any excuse to throw a party! But I waited until the summer so that the entire menu could be made from local ingredients, many of them nurtured, grown, and raised by the very people now sitting around the table. Of course, the group was limited by logistics and schedules. So many people have contributed to both this book and to Slow Food in our state that I would have needed to rent a gymnasium for the whole crowd. But as it turned out, the party was just the right size for sitting together and sharing memories.

"Well, I grew up on a small dairy farm in northern New Jersey," recalled Matt Systema, chef at George Rude's Griggstown Quail Farm. "Basically all our family meals came from our own farm." He still gets a rush of nostalgia when he eats food that's been grown the right way. And that night, it seemed to me that Matt was getting a little dreamy-eyed as he dug into the kale cooked with ham hocks. "To me, Slow Food is all about the importance of tradition," he continued. "I used to take tradition for granted, but now I really see the value of a meal around the family table, shared by the people who matter to you the most."

"Oh, I know just what you mean," said Pegi Ballister-Howells. She recalled how her father always needed a big bowl of greens at every dinner. "He would have loved this kale," she said. Then she laughed and told us that sometimes her husband, Tom, comes home, takes a deep breath, and says, "It smells just like Nana's house." What he means is that Pegi's cooking has stirred memories of his own family meals; and when that happens, Pegi joked, "I know I can get anything I want from him!" But she and her family also understand that a good meal enjoyed together is the most important thing they can do as a family. The cherished memories they are making will linger with the next generation.

Pat Tanner told our group, "It didn't take me long to figure out that food writing is really about people." Recently, she's starting noticing that all her food assignments have really been about the people behind the food. She's especially proud of what she's written about Slow Food and believes that we all became involved in the movement for the right reasons. Even early on, "we knew the value of what Slow Food meant," Pat said that night. "It was a magical experi-

Food sign on the street outside the Brothers Moon Restaurant in Hopewell, New Jersey

Photo by Jim Weaver

ence, and the events that we put on were unprecedented. Everybody was doing food-tasting events, but nobody was pairing farmers with the chefs. The fact that that was happening in my home town of Princeton was unbelievable to me. It was inconceivable that I would be able to get actual authentic food around here, like the kind Jim was preparing at Tre Piani. But we did—and that was all that really mattered."

I couldn't let the evening pass without adding my own memories. "Conviviality is really the reason that I became a chef and restaurateur," I told the group. "I've always enjoyed cooking for others—I guess because I enjoy the company of my friends and family so much." Until recently, I hadn't realized how much writing this book had made me ponder my own journey as a chef and a Slow Food supporter. Thinking back to my early years, I suddenly saw that my upbringing and my family had prepared me for my career in the hospitality business. After all, what is hospitality if not the satisfaction of bringing people together to enjoy good food and drink and to promote conviviality?

Lessons from My Father

Years ago, my father offered some valuable insight into my new career. He is an architect, and he pointed out that in his business he had to spend long periods of time with clients before he could achieve final results. "But in your restaurant business," he said, "you get your results over and over again, every day and every night." I think he hit on something that's a real draw for chefs: the rush that comes when you put your heart and soul into something that brings pleasure to others and that you also know has properly nourished them. Looking back, I see that my instincts have always fit perfectly with the Slow Food message.

Like many of the others who were sitting around the table that night, my family was a big inspiration in my career choice. I, too, am a New Jersey kid. I grew up in a beautiful rural area of trees and rolling hills and farmlands. Nobody in our family ever questioned why New Jersey's motto was "the Garden State." Though my family was fairly small, we all loved to entertain and enjoyed bountiful meals, whether they were just among ourselves or special celebrations for holidays or birthdays. Our passion for get-togethers was probably enhanced by the fact that my grandparents, my cousins, and my parents all lived within twenty minutes of one another. We weren't *too* close. (Just as "good fences make good neighbors," a little distance makes for happy extended families.) But we were definitely close enough to get a party going. Wherever we gathered, we made the occasion an event, and the results were always memorable.

Both of my parents were good cooks. But while my mother always cooked a darn good meal, she didn't get as much pleasure from cooking as my father did. (I think my chef's DNA comes from Dad.) She did, however, instill in my sisters and me the pleasure of sitting at the dinner table. To this day, we all look forward to getting together for meals.

My father loves to cook and to eat. He especially enjoys cooking for a crowd, and he can come up with any excuse to invite people over. If Slow Food didn't already have a conviviality manifesto, I think my father would have volunteered to invent one. He is the essence of conviviality. Instinctively, he knows that most the important part of an evening is the camaraderie, not how fancy the food is or how many different kinds of dishes sit on the table. He's never even too worried about whether people like his cooking.

I cherish the memory of how happy my father was to cook for the many parties that he and my mother threw. Whatever his dishes may have lacked in flavor they made up for in abundance. And whatever was on our table was always seasoned by my parents' generosity and welcoming spirit. My father even enjoyed shopping for food. Odds were that, if my mother asked him to pick up a gallon of milk, he would walk back into the house with the milk plus with ten or fifteen bags full of "necessities" such as sweetbreads, a dozen kinds of cold cuts, and three kinds of bread. Over his shoulder might be slung a bag of in-season apples or a fresh packet of shad roe. "Well, after all," he would say, "they're only in season for a short time. And since we need a gallon of milk now, we might as well have three for later!"

The cooking bug bit me at a young age, and I always knew there would be enough food in the family pantry to experiment on. It didn't take people long to see that I was getting pretty good at the job, too. I remember one early kitchen adventure, when I cooked a Long Island duck that my father had purchased on one of his excursions. I was only about fifteen years old, and my guests were a couple of buddies. We were famished from riding our bikes all over creation that day. "What can you cook for us?" one of them asked. Even at age fifteen, my chef's reputation was growing.

"Well," I replied, "how about roast duck à l'orange with wild rice and fresh asparagus?" That's how a future chef talks.

But as much as I love cooking, to me, the great food I was able to serve at the Slow Food party was just a bonus. The gift was being able to have the party at all. In other words, the people come first—another lesson I learned from my father. When I was a young boy, he and I joined a father-son group called the Indian Guides. My name was Little Deer. My father was Big Wind. (If you've ever seen him, you might have an inkling why.) Each month our group would meet for an hour or so to discuss important "tribal matters" at members' homes. Those summits were usually enhanced with plates of store-bought cookies and juice in little paper cups. But not at our house. Whenever it was our turn to host, the meetings turned out quite differently.

First of all, forget the meeting: we had a full-fledged party. Those little paper cups of juice? They were replaced with a full bar (for the grownups, not the kids, of course). Plates of cookies? No way. We plowed into platters of barbecued chicken, ribs, corn on the cob, Jersey tomatoes, and whatever else my father decided to serve that day. He always made sure there was dessert for the kids and cigars for the fathers as well as plenty of time to run around and work off everything we had just wolfed down. Needless to say, attendance was pretty high at our "meetings."

If You Have Food, They Will Come

Whatever the gathering, food connects people. Is it any wonder we in the Slow Food movement are so passionate about wanting that food to be the best and most wholesome we can offer? If family and friends are important, if we truly love them, why should we be content to nourish them with food that is haphazard and artificial? Think about it: in life, there are only two truly sensual experiences, and only one of them can be enjoyed publicly. To share truly good food with your fellow human beings is a joy that encompasses all the senses. Not for nothing does the phrase "to break bread" with someone conjure up an image of peace and understanding. "To break bread" means to lay aside one's differences and share a universal delight.

So in the end, everything goes back to conviviality. I thought about that truth as I sat at my midsummer banquet, loving my friends, remembering my family, and appreciating how Slow Food has touched all of us. That night, we hoped that my book would widen our circle of friends and colleagues and inspire more people to join us in the Slow Food experience. I hope you're one of them! Whether you join officially or just by way of the choices you make to support wholesome, authentic, sustainable food, we welcome you.

We always have room for more at our table.

ૐ

Slow Food Dinner

Tre Piani, July 15, 2010

Cape May Salt oysters on the half shell with cilantro mignonette
Viking Village big-eye tuna tartare
Viking Village sea scallops with pignolia nut crust
Quick pickles stuffed with free-range egg salad
Valley Shepherd Oldwick Shepherd cheese
Cherry Grove tomme
Salumeria Biellese finochietta and soppressata
Salumeria Biellese prosciutto with grilled peaches
Mr. McGregor's baby greens salad
Rutgers tomatoes and fresh basil
Oak Grove plantation polenta
Local kale with Cherry Grove ham hocks
Viking Village tilefish with garlic and herbs
Griggstown Farm chicken with red wine
Rigatoni with Kennett Square exotic mushrooms
Warm peach strudel
Dried cranberry biscotti

19

Off the Soap Box
and onto the Chapters

It's great to see people's eyes light up when they taste the "real thing" at a farm-to-table Slow Food event. As they crunch into a right-off-the-farm asparagus stalk or bite into a garden-fresh blueberry, even sixty-year-olds can look like kids. But where can the uninitiated become part of the Slow Food experience? Your best bet is an event sponsored by a local chapter. Here's a sample of what several Slow Food chapters in the tri-state region have offered recently. Each chapter has its own distinct personality and appeal, and I hope that their lively and innovative events will make you want to get involved in your local chapter and learn more about the Slow Food experience. (A list of chapter websites appears in the Resource section.)

Slow Food Northern New Jersey

"Redefining a Garden State of Mind" is the theme of this Slow Food chapter. As its website states, "through Slow Food NNJ initiatives, such as food tasting and seminars, cooking demonstrations, farm tours, school food garden programs, and much more, residents will develop a real taste for our state and find themselves in a Garden State of Mind." Slow Food Northern New Jersey also focuses on the younger generation. In August 2010, for instance, it hosted a benefit for school kids at Fosterfields Living Historical Farm in Morristown, New Jersey, which operates just as farms did at the turn of the twentieth century. The August event, called a "Sustenance on the Farm" dinner, featured locally produced food and wine and even a fiddle player.

Slow Food Central New Jersey

You have already read about some of the events organized by my own local chapter, and all I can add is that we intend to keep planting the seeds for more fans of local foods and traditions. As the chapter's founder, organizer, and all-around go-to guy, I invite you to join us.

The dynamic of our chapter has changed over the years. Although we reduced our roster of events during the recession, we intend to keep moving ahead with new members and old friends. In the past we have organized large festivals at local wineries that drew thousands of people from all over the tri-state area. We have also organized very small events that included small dinners at area restaurants, potluck dinners at member's homes, and even a tasting of tea and chocolate. One of our longest-running and most popular events is our series of winter farmers' markets, which take place indoors once a month in December, January, and February. Venues for these markets include Tre Piani, the Museum of Agriculture at Rutgers, and the D and R Greenway Trust in Princeton.

Slow Food South Jersey

South Jersey is home to one of the nation's most bountiful seafood lockers—the confluence of the Delaware Bay and the Atlantic Ocean—and this Slow Food chapter offers plenty of lively opportunities to learn more about the region's foodstuffs. Its website includes a wealth of practical, detailed information about local farmers' markets and CSAs as well as Slow Food chefs such as Chris Huber and Lucas Manteca, who both cook in the Cape May area. It provides links to interesting businesses and organizations such as the Cape May County Beach Plum Association, Bill's Bees, and Niblock's Pork Store. The chapter also keeps track of legislative news impacting local agriculture and offers access to a local farmers' blog.

Slow Food Philadelphia

This chapter plays up conviviality, which is one of the pillars of the Slow Food movement. According to its website, "our chapter comes together regularly to share at organized dinners, tastings, tours, and picnics. We also lend support to local organizations and initiatives in our area that promote the richness of our area's culinary heritage."

Slow Food Philadelphia has always been an active chapter. Given the city's proximity to so much rich farmland, it's no wonder that many residents, students, and food and beverage professionals have answered the movement's call. The chapter has offered educational seminars on all kinds of food-related subjects,

A great convivial meal in Siena, Italy, with Jim, Kim,
Chef Pietro, and Siena Slow Food leader Marco Becchi

including a garlic tasting and two of the city's favorite fermentations: cheese and
beer. If you ever get a chance to taste a few local beers, I have a feeling you will
understand why these events are so popular. In the summer of 2010, the chapter
sponsored its sixth annual fundraiser: "Good Food, Good Beer, and the Rest Is
History." City restaurants such as Fork and Noble prepared signature dishes
using local meats, produce, and cheeses and paired them with great local beers
from area breweries such as the Philadelphia Brewing Company and Victory.

Slow Food NYC

The city that never sleeps has a Slow Food chapter that never stops. You can tell
as much from its website, which is packed with information about a lively stream
of events, programs, and innovations. One of the most intriguing is the chapter's
"directory of the restaurants, bars, food and beverage artisans, and stores and
markets that, because of their contributions to the quality, authenticity, and sus-

tainability of the food supply of the City of New York, have been awarded the SFNYC Snail of Approval." Anyone can nominate an establishment for the Snail of Approval directory; but to earn a place on the list, it must follow the guidelines of the Slow Food message, which is to support a food economy that is "good, clean, and fair." The chapter identifies three criteria: quality ("Food must taste good and be good for us"), authenticity ("Food [must be] true to its source"), and sustainability ("We must pay attention to the consequences of how we produce and distribute food"). The chapter also encourages supporters to "contact us about holding an educational tasting at your favorite ethnic restaurant, or take us on a walking-tour of a culinary-rich neighborhood, or help us to organize a volunteer-day at one of the city's farms."

Slow Food Hudson Valley

Slow Food Hudson Valley works to appeal to every kind of Slow Food member, from foodies to politicos. Its website gives prominent space to political and regulatory issues such the "No Farms, No Food" rally in early 2010, which protested state budget cuts for environmental and agricultural programs. The chapter urges members to contact the Department of Agriculture to protest a draft of an environmental impact statement that gives a pass to genetically engineered alfalfa, and it provides links to sites devoted to issues such as water rights, food safety, and toxic cosmetics. Hudson Valley also promotes lively events and programs, including the Eat Local Food movement, which encourages people to buy food that's been produced within a 100-mile radius. It features farm-to-table events and practical cooking classes for Slow Food newcomers. "With a few tips and recipes," the website promises, "you'll be able to take full advantage of all the seasonal produce your local markets have to offer."

⁊

Kim's favorite kind of farm

Photo by Jim Weaver

As a farewell gift, I want to share a couple of recipes from one of America's most celebrated chefs, Michael Anthony of Gramercy Tavern in New York City. Enjoy!

Hot Smoked Brook Trout, Asparagus Puree, and Pickled Cippollini Onions

Serves 4

ASPARAGUS PUREE:

1 cup asparagus stems, thinly sliced
1 cup vegetable stock
1 cup cippollini onions, peeled and sliced
1 shallot, minced
1 garlic clove, minced
1 tbsp. water
1 tbsp. butter
Sea salt
Freshly ground black pepper

PICKLED CIPPOLLINI ONIONS:

1 star anise
2 beets
2 tbsp. red verjus (pressed juice of unripened grapes; available in specialty food stores)
1 cup white-wine vinegar
½ cup water
1 tbsp. sugar
1 tsp. sea salt
4 cippollini onions, peeled and sliced into rings

PICKLED ONION VINAIGRETTE:

1 small beet
1 cup good-quality red wine
1 medium-sized onion, peeled and minced
1 tbsp. raspberry vinegar
1 tbsp. red-wine vinegar
1 tbsp. port
½ cup extra-virgin olive oil
Lemon juice

BROOK TROUT:

4 6-ounce brook trout fillets
Sea salt
Freshly ground black pepper

FOR THE ASPARAGUS PUREE: Blanch the asparagus for 1 minute, drain, and plunge it into an ice bath. Drain. In a blender, puree the asparagus with the vegetable stock until smooth.

Gently cook the onions, shallots, and garlic over medium heat. When they are translucent but still have no color, add the water and cook the vegetables for about 10 minutes or until they are tender.

Meanwhile, in a small heavy pan, cook the butter slowly over medium heat until it begins to turn brown. Add the vegetables and the brown butter to the asparagus puree in the blender. Pulse until smooth. Add salt and pepper to taste.

FOR THE PICKLED CIPPOLLINI ONIONS: Put the beets into a large saucepan, cover with water, and bring to a boil. Reduce heat to a simmer, and cook until tender, from 30 minutes to 1 hour, depending on the size and age of the beets. Cool under running water. Slip off the skins, trim the ends, and dice.

Toast the star anise in a medium-sized saucepan over medium heat until they begin to let off a stronger aroma, about 2 minutes. Add beets, red verjus, white wine vinegar, water, sugar, and salt. Bring to a simmer, then strain. Throw away the solids, keeping only the liquid. Add cippollini onions, and chill. (This preparation preserves the onions and will hold for several weeks in the refrigerator.)

PICKLED ONION VINAIGRETTE: Cook the beet according to the instructions in the previous section. After peeling and trimming it, drop it into a blender or a juicer, and puree. Then strain the juice through a fine mesh strainer.

Pour the red wine into a small saucepan, and cook it over medium heat until it has reduced to 1 tbsp.

Combine onion, beet juice, raspberry vinegar, red-wine vinegar, red-wine reduction, and port in a medium-sized saucepan over medium heat. Bring to a simmer, and cook until the onion is tender and the liquid has reduced by about half. Finish the vinaigrette by whisking in the olive oil and a drop of lemon juice.

TO COOK THE TROUT: Preheat one side of an outdoor gas grill to medium-high. Line the opposite side with aluminum foil. Add a handful of applewood chips to the heated side, and place the trout fillets skin side down on the foil. Close the lid, and let the fillets cook through slowly, 7 to 10 minutes. Remove the trout from the grill, let cool, and remove the skin and any rough edges. Season to taste with salt and pepper.

TO ASSEMBLE THE DISH: Spoon the asparagus puree onto the center of the dish. Streak one side of the plate with the pickled cippollini onions and the other side with the onion vinaigrette. Place the smoked trout fillet on top of the asparagus puree.

Whole Spelt Spaghetti with Navy Beans, Ramps, and My Grandfather's Garlic

Serves 6 generously

WHOLE SPELT SPAGHETTI:

1 pound plus 3 ounces bread flour (also known as high-gluten flour)

1 pound spelt flour (available in specialty markets)

¾ tsp. kosher salt

8 eggs

6 egg yolks

NAVY BEANS:

2 cups organic dry navy beans (or substitute dry Great Northern beans)

1 medium-sized Spanish onion, peeled and finely chopped

1 stalk celery, finely chopped

1 carrot, peeled and finely chopped

3 cloves garlic, peeled and finely chopped

2 Tbsp. extra-virgin olive oil

1 bay leaf

Water

Sea salt

Freshly ground black pepper

RAMPS:

1 bunch (25–30) ramps, washed, trimmed, and thinly sliced

2 tbsp. extra-virgin olive oil

MY GRANDFATHER'S GARLIC:

1 whole head of garlic, peeled and the cloves thinly sliced

2 cups peanut oil

Fine sea salt

MIXED HERBS AND OLIVE OIL FINISH:

1 tsp. tarragon, finely chopped

1 tsp. basil, finely chopped

1 tsp. chives, finely chopped

Extra-virgin olive oil

FOR THE SPAGHETTI: In an electric mixer with a dough hook, combine the pasta ingredients until they form a dough. Using a pasta machine, roll the dough until it is very thin. If you do not have a pasta machine, roll the dough into thin sheets about 6 inches wide and 18 inches long. Dust them with flour, and place up to four sheets directly on top of each other. Roll up the pile of sheets so that they look like a roll of paper towels. Then cut the roll into ⅛-inch-thick slices. Shake out the cut pasta into long strands. Dust them with all-purpose flour, and lay them out on a cookie sheet until ready to cook. The pasta should be cooked the same day it is made.

FOR THE NAVY BEANS: Pour the navy beans into a large bowl, cover them with water at least 2 inches above the level of the beans, and soak them overnight. Drain before using.

In a large stockpot over low heat, cook the onion, celery, carrot, and garlic in olive oil until the vegetables are soft but not colored. Add the beans and the bay leaf as well as enough water to cover the contents of the pot. Bring to a boil. Then reduce the heat and simmer the mixture for 35 minutes or until the beans are just tender. Remove from heat, and season with salt and pepper. Set aside. (The beans can be made several days ahead if kept refrigerated.) Reheat before serving.

FOR THE RAMPS: Lightly cook in olive oil in a medium sauté pan over low heat until the ramps begin to sweat. Remove from heat, and reserve at room temperature.

FOR MY GRANDFATHER'S GARLIC: Bring about 2 quarts of lightly salted water to a boil in a medium-sized saucepan. Drop the garlic into the boiling water, and cook for about 1 minute. Remove with a strainer or slotted spoon and repeat the blanching process two more times. Dry the slices on a kitchen towel, and let them sit at room temperature so that any remaining water evaporates, about 5 minutes.

Pour the peanut oil into a medium-sized saucepan, and heat until a frying thermometer reads 350 degrees. Be careful not to let the oil smoke. Add the garlic slices to the hot oil, and stir lightly to be sure they do not stick together, about 2 minutes. With a slotted spoon, remove the garlic to a cookie sheet lined with paper towels, and season lightly with salt. Hold at room temperature until ready to use.

TO ASSEMBLE THE DISH: Cook the spaghetti in a large pot of lightly salted boiling water for about 2 minutes. Drain. Combine the hot spaghetti with the ramps and the mixed chopped herbs.

To serve, spoon the warm beans, with a generous amount of cooking liquid, into a bowl. Top with spaghetti and ramps. Drizzle with olive oil and sprinkle with the fried garlic.

ᔰ RESOURCES

Slow Food Northern New Jersey
   http://www.slowfoodnnj.org

Slow Food Central New Jersey
   http://www.slowfoodcentralnj.org

Slow Food South Jersey
   http://slowfood-sj.org

Slow Food Philadelphia
   http://www.slowfoodphilly.org

Slow Food NYC
   http://www.slowfoodnyc.org

Slow Food Hudson Valley
   http://www.slowfoodhv.org

Appendix
The Slow Food Manifesto

The Slow Food international movement officially began when delegates from fifteen countries endorsed the following manifesto, written by founding member Folco Portinari, on December 10, 1989.

- Our century, which began and has developed under the insignia of industrial civilization, first invented the machine and then took it as its life model.

- We are enslaved by speed and have all succumbed to the same insidious virus: Fast Life, which disrupts our habits, pervades the privacy of our homes, and forces us to eat Fast Foods.

- To be worthy of the name, *Homo sapiens* should rid himself of speed before it reduces him to a species in danger of extinction.

- A firm defense of quiet material pleasure is the only way to oppose the universal folly of Fast Life.

- May suitable doses of guaranteed sensual pleasure and slow, long-lasting enjoyment preserve us from the contagion of the multitude who mistake frenzy for efficiency.

- Our defense should begin at the table with Slow Food.

- Let us rediscover the flavors and savors of regional cooking and banish the degrading effects of Fast Food.

- In the name of productivity, Fast Life has changed our way of being and threatens our environment and our landscapes. So Slow Food is now the only truly progressive answer.

- That is what real culture is all about: developing taste rather than demeaning it. And what better way to set about this than an international exchange of experiences, knowledge, projects?

- Slow Food guarantees a better future. Slow Food is an idea that needs plenty of qualified supporters who can help turn this (slow) motion into an international movement, with the little snail as its symbol.

About the Author

JIM WEAVER is chef and owner of Tre Piani in Princeton, New Jersey, one of the best-known Italian restaurants in the state. The founder of Slow Food Central New Jersey, Jim has run some of the top professional kitchens in New Jersey and has also worked in Italy and the Caribbean. He recently served on the board of directors for the New Jersey Restaurant Association and is affiliated with countless professional organizations and charity events.